SOLVING CRIMES

PIONEERS OF FORENSIC SCIENCE

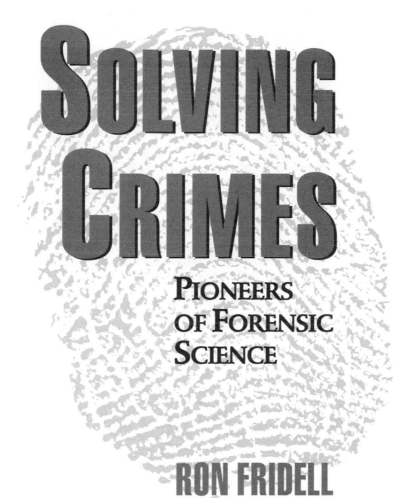

SOLVING CRIMES

PIONEERS OF FORENSIC SCIENCE

RON FRIDELL

Lives in Science

FRANKLIN WATTS
A Division of Grolier Publishing
New York • London • Hong Kong • Sydney
Danbury, Connecticut

Cover design by Dave Klaboe   Interior design by Molly Heron

Illustration created by George Stewart

Photographs ©: AP/Wide World Photos: 79, 83, 85, 91; Brown Brothers: 33; Corbis-Bettmann: 31 (Hulton-Deutsch Collection), 18, 26, 58; Culver Pictures: 14, 23, 52; Eric Stoves: 94; Globe Photos: 113; Liaison Agency Inc.: 60 (Goivaux Agency/Rapho), cover center (Jeremy Bigwood), 97 (George De Keerle), 41 (Hulton Getty); National Library of Medicine: 55, 65; North Wind Picture Archives: 69, 87; Photo Researchers: 30 (Scott Camazine), 108 (Neville Chadwick/SPL), 73 (Science Photo Library), cover bottom (David Parker/SPL), 43 (Mary Evans Picture Library); Tony Stone Images: cover background (Laurence Dutton), 106 (David Joel), cover top (Don Spiro).

Visit Franklin Watts on the Internet at:
http://publishing.grolier.com

Library of Congress Cataloging-in-Publication Data

Fridell, Ron.
    Solving crimes: pioneers of forensic science / by Ron Fridell.
        p.   cm.—(Lives in Science)
    Includes bibliographical references and index.
    Summary: Profiles the work of six individuals whose work shaped the field of forensic science: Alphonse Bertillon, Edward Henry, Karl Landsteiner, Edmond Locard, Clyde Snow, and Alec Jeffreys.
    ISBN 0-531-11721-9
    1. Forensic scientists—Biography—Juvenile literature. 2. Forensic science—History—Juvenile literature. 3. Criminal investigation—History—Juvenile literature. [1. Forensic scientists. 2. Forensic sciences. 3. Criminal investigation.] I. Title. II. Series.
HV8073.8.F75   2000
363.25'092'2—dc21   99-13381
[B]   CIP
                                                                AC

© 2000 Franklin Watts, a Division of Grolier Publishing
All rights reserved. Published simultaneously in Canada.
Printed in the United States of America.
1 2 3 4 5 6 7 8 9 10 R 09 08 07 06 05 04 03 02 01 00

CONTENTS

SOLVING CRIMES

PIONEERS OF FORENSIC SCIENCE

INTRODUCTION

- As a burglar flees from the scene of a crime, he vaults over a high iron fence with spikes on top. A ring on one finger gets caught on a spike, and he is forced to leave the finger behind.

- A murderer kills his victim in a flour mill.

- A killer leaves traces of *semen* on the clothing of his victims.

Each of these criminals was caught because he left something behind—or took something with him. Thanks to forensic science, these three criminals were brought to justice by a fingerprint, a particle of dust, and a few cells. Forensic scientists use virtually all the other sciences—including biology, botany, entomology, zoology, anthropology, psychiatry, medicine, statistics, and physics—to develop new techniques for discovering, identifying, and comparing physical evidence.

This book profiles six pioneers of forensic science—from Alphonse Bertillon who was born in 1853 to Alec Jeffreys who was born nearly 100 years later. By examining the careers and lives of important forensic scientists, this book traces the explosive growth of this many-faceted science. It also shows how each of the scientists managed to overcome formidable obstacles through sheer determination and an ingenious instinct for seeing things in startling new ways.

This book also focuses on the methods the pioneers of forensic science developed to determine human identity. Some of their techniques are simple, while others are quite complex. They range from measuring a person's height to analyzing the structure of a person's *molecules*. The goal of all these methods is to determine what makes each of us unique.

Although these forensic pioneers were different in many ways, they shared a passion for order. Science gives us a sense that we can grasp anything—even things we cannot see. Forensic scientists make sense out of confusing information and evidence every day. They do this by breaking things down into their component parts and then classifying those components. In this way, they help to make the mysterious understandable.

Most of the people described in this book are men because, until fairly recently, men dominated the fields of science and law. Today, however, careers in forensic science are open to men and women alike. More than half a dozen major universities now offer degrees in some aspect of forensic science. A typical state forensic crime laboratory works on more than 75,000 cases a year and employs more than 200 scientists, technicians, and support staff.

This army of forensic scientists and technicians is dedicated to collecting, analyzing, and interpreting evidence. The evidence is used not only to convict the guilty, but also to clear people accused of crimes they did not commit. Justice is the goal, not punishment.

To obtain justice, law enforcement officials are relying more and more on forensic evidence, and with good reason. Historically, eyewitness accounts in criminal cases have proved notoriously unreliable and often misleading. The memory of a human being is subjective. Different people often see the same event in significantly different ways, and some witnesses deliberately lie about what they observed. But fingerprints don't lie; nor do bones or hair or dust or blood. Forensic evidence is objective evidence. If properly obtained and correctly interpreted, it can be consistently relied upon in criminal cases.

Forensic evidence has not always been seen in a positive light, however. This book details the skeptical stance both the law-enforcement and legal communities have taken toward every new advance in forensic science. But despite so much criticism, the men described in this book persisted. In time, their patience and passion paid off.

CHAPTER 1
"A REVOLUTION IN POLICE WORK"

Alphonse Bertillon and the
Art of Measuring Criminals

Time was running out. Just a few precious days remained for a file clerk named Alphonse Bertillon to prove that his system for keeping track of criminals—a system his superiors called "a joke"—would forever revolutionize police work.

It was February 20, 1883. For the last 4 years, Bertillon had toiled away unnoticed in a remote corner of police headquarters in Paris, France. In the summer, Bertillon's little corner was hot and stuffy. In the winter, it turned so chilly that he wore gloves to keep his fingers from freezing.

These were far from ideal conditions for conducting a historic scientific experiment. But for the last few months, Bertillon had been doing just that. Every day, dozens of criminals were brought to him: a motley parade of thieves, counterfeiters, terrorists, cutthroats, and murderers. The police asked each man for his name, but there was no way to know whether the criminal was giving his real name or an alias.

Armed with a ruler, a tape measure, and *calipers,* Bertillon and his two assistants recorded each man's physical measurements. They made eleven separate measurements in all, including the height of his body, the length of his forearms, and the thickness of his head. Each measurement was taken three times. The results were then averaged and the criminal classified as either small, medium, or large for each measurement.

Bertillon carefully recorded this meticulously gathered information on index cards, which were then filed in an archive. By looking through the archive, any clerk trained in Bertillon's system could quickly and easily determine whether a newly measured criminal had ever been arrested before.

Bertillon's system of criminal identification, known as *anthropometry,* was based on three assumptions:

- After age 20, the dimensions of the bones that make up the human skeleton do not change.

- According to the mathematics of probability, the chance of two adults having the same value for two of the eleven measurements was 16 to 1.

- The chance of two adults having the same value for all eleven measurements was 4,191,304 to 1.

Bertillon had devised this system for identifying criminals 4 years earlier—soon after he began working at police headquarters. He had been struggling to get permission to test his system ever since. Request after request had been filed, and request after request had been denied.

Why? His superiors thought of police work as an art—not a science. In Bertillon's time, detectives couldn't imagine science playing a key role in solving crimes. They depended on subjective intuition and cunning, not on objective scientific methods. The microscope was not

Frenchman Alphonse Bertillon developed the first successful system for identifying criminals.

yet seen as a tool for tracking down criminals, and *blood typing* had yet to be discovered.

Through years of dogged persistence Bertillon had succeeded in persuading his boss, Prefect of Police Jean Camecasse, to give anthropometry a chance. In November 1882, Camecasse grudgingly granted Bertillon 3 months to prove that anthropometry was a foolproof system for identifying criminals. Beginning on December 1, each arrested criminal was brought to Bertillon for measurement.

From the beginning, Bertillon knew that success depended upon finding a repeat offender. In other words, at least one criminal would have to be caught, measured by Bertillon, serve his jail sentence, be released, and then be caught committing another crime, and be re-measured. Only then could the criminal be positively identified as the same man who had committed the previous crime. And all this would have to happen within 3 months.

By February 20, 1883, Bertillon and his two assistants had processed more than 1,800 criminals. They had yet to find a single repeat offender. Bertillon had only 9 days left to prove that his system worked. Bertillon had done all he could. What he needed now—needed desperately—was a stroke of luck. Would he get a lucky break?

Alphonse Bertillon was a man who seemed destined for failure from the start. Born in 1853, he had been an unhealthy child. His headaches, nosebleeds, and poor digestion only worsened with age. An unruly child and a poor student, Alphonse was expelled from some of the best schools in France.

Bad-tempered, arrogant, and sarcastic, Alphonse grew into a man who was virtually friendless. With his thin face, sad eyes, and expressionless voice, he was not a likable person.

But Alphonse was blessed with a strong and loving father who refused to give up on his son. A distinguished physician, Dr. Louis Adolphe Bertillon was also Vice President of the Anthropological Society of Paris. Alphonse's grandfather, Achille Grillard, was also a scientist—a renowned *naturalist* and mathematician. In the Bertillon household, science was something to be lived and breathed. The young Alphonse had heard all about the leading scientists of the time. He was familiar with Charles Darwin's *theory of evolution,* Louis Pasteur's pioneering work with *microorganisms,* George Cuvier's eye-opening work with dinosaur bones, and French physicist Louis Daguerre's revolutionary work with photography.

These scientists believed that life's problems could be solved by applying the *scientific method.* In the Bertillon household, the scientific method was practiced daily. For years, visitors to the Bertillon home were measured, head to toe, as the young Alphonse looked on. His father and grandfather recorded their visitors' measurements in order to test an intriguing *hypothesis* advanced by Belgian astronomer and statistician Adolphe Quetelet.

Nature exhibited an infinite variety of forms, Quetelet wrote. So great was that variety, he hypothesized, that no two persons with identical physical measurements would ever be found. After years of measuring their visitors and comparing the results, Alphonse's father and grandfather had to agree. No two people were exactly alike. And the closer you looked at them, the more differences you saw.

Unfortunately, the grown-up Alphonse had a difficult time putting his scientific background to practical use. He served a brief apprenticeship at a bank, then worked in England as a tutor for a short time before returning to

Paris. He seemed too stubborn and disagreeable to ever hold a job for long. It took all of his father's influence to get Alphonse a low-level job as assistant file clerk at police headquarters in Paris.

On March 15, 1879, at the age of 26, Alphonse Bertillon began his job. He worked in the archives designed to keep track of Paris's known criminals. All the information that police gathered in the course of arrests and interrogations was stored here.

The information dated back nearly 70 years. In 1810, Emperor Napoleon Bonaparte had appointed a man known as Monsieur Henry as the head of the French police. Bonaparte ordered Henry to find a way to decrease crime in France, and especially in Paris.

Before Bonaparte came to power, violent crime was an accepted part of life in Paris. Wealthy aristocrats lived in constant fear. Criminals often broke into their homes in broad daylight and took whatever they pleased. With Bonaparte in power, the criminals of Paris had to go underground.

Monsieur Henry and his men were good at their work, but the criminals of Paris were better. Things got so bad that Monsieur Henry decided to try something radical. He hired Eugene Francois Vidocq—the most famous criminal in Paris. As a veteran thief and escape artist, Vidocq knew more about how crimes were committed—and who committed them—than anyone else in Paris. Vidocq was hungry for power, and he wanted revenge against other Parisian criminals.

Vidocq proved to be an inspired choice. His organization, which was composed of former convicts, arrested 812 criminals the first year. Vidocq managed this by planting his men in prisons. Masquerading as prisoners, they were able to gather inside information about the criminal community.

Paris's Eugene Francois Vidocq—master criminal turned master detective

Vidocq himself proved to be a formidable crime fighter. He regularly visited prison yards and had criminals march in a circle around him. As they marched, he would watch their faces. Vidocq had a photographic memory for faces as well as firsthand knowledge of how criminals operated. He also knew where their hideouts were located. Vidocq's methods for fighting crime were followed for many years.

Building an archive of criminals' descriptions had been Vidocq's idea. He had hired an army of clerks to maintain the archive. But by the late 1800s, when Bertillon began working at police headquarters, Vidocq's methods seemed old-fashioned. Society had changed, and so had the nature of crime. Criminals were smarter than they had been in the early 1800s. In addition, because the criminal population had grown right along with the general population, the archive had grown tremendously. It now contained nearly 5 million descriptions.

These descriptions were organized according to the criminals' last names. Bertillon immediately realized that this was a bad idea. He knew that criminals seldom gave their real names. They used a different alias each time they were arrested. Another was the photographs filed with the descriptions. They had been shot from all sorts of different distances and angles. Some were out of focus, others were badly lit. And the criminals had been allowed to grin and distort their faces in front of the camera. Worst of all, the descriptions were written with imprecise words such as "tall," "thin," and "ordinary."

As Bertillon filed paperwork in the archives, he thought of all the measurements his father and grandfather had taken over the years. Why write "tall" to describe a man's height when you could note the exact length in meters and centimeters? Why write "medium" to describe a man's head when you could measure its dimensions exactly? Why not apply anthropometry to police work?

Bertillon discussed his revolutionary idea with his father. "It will mean a revolution in police work," his father told him. "You will teach the police of France the meaning of scientific work."[1]

So Bertillon put his concerns into a written report to his superiors. Could he be granted permission to take the measurements of the criminals who were brought into police headquarters and create a new archive? If Bertillon had been as good a writer as he was a thinker, he might have had immediate success. But the report he submitted was impossible to read. His thoughts were clear enough in his own mind, but when he wrote them down they became muddy and confused.

But Bertillon would not quit. At his father's urging, he kept filing request after request. Finally, his boss, Camecasse, gave him a chance. Now Bertillon had only 9 days to find a repeat offender. Otherwise, his system of anthropometry would be labeled a failure.

Bertillon was getting worried, but he continued to hope for the best. When an officer brought him a criminal named Dupont, a light went on inside Bertillon's head. This was not the first time this criminal had crossed his path. He was certain he'd seen this man before. And that meant that Dupont's description was somewhere among the more than 1,800 index cards he'd filed away over the past few months. This was the moment Bertillon had been waiting for. Would he be able to prove the value of his system?

Bertillon carefully took the man's measurements. He was sure that the name the criminal had given was an alias. Nearly all criminals in Paris gave false names to avoid detection, and "Dupont" was a particularly popular choice at the moment. Criminals also knew other ways to fool police using the old archive. For example, they often grew a beard or a mustache—or shaved them off—to alter their appearance. But Bertillon knew that the criminals couldn't fool him. After all, a person can't alter the thickness of his head, the distance between his eyes, or the length of his left foot.

When Bertillon finished measuring Dupont, he searched through the archive for a set of measurements that matched. The process went like this: The width of Dupont's head put him into the "medium" category. This immediately eliminated more than half of the criminals Bertillon had measured. The width of his head further narrowed the search, and the length of his middle finger narrowed it even more. The length of his little finger cut the search down to a single file that held fifty descriptions. It took Bertillon only a few minutes more to find the index card he was looking for.

Yes, he had indeed seen this man before. The information on an index card labeled "Martin" matched Dupont's measurements exactly.

"You were arrested for stealing on December 15 of last year," Bertillon informed him. "At that time you called yourself Martin."[2]

Faced with objective evidence he could not deny, the man confessed. When Camecasse heard the news, he agreed to allow Bertillon to continue his experiments in anthropometry. Bertillon's revolutionary system led to another 26 positive identifications in 1883, and 300 in 1884. By then, the unruly and unpleasant Alphonse Bertillon was known far and wide as the first man to successfully apply the scientific method to *criminology*.

To honor him, journalists renamed this system *bertillonage*. Headlines in Paris newspapers hailed his achievements. One read, "Young French Scientist Revolutionizes the Identification of Criminals." Another announced, "French Police Once Again Lead the Way for the World."

Bertillon's work provided the basis for many new systems of classification. All were based upon breaking down large amounts of information into smaller groups in order to narrow the field of search.

Bertillon kept hard at work refining his system. This exacting scientist demanded that the photographing of criminals be strictly standardized. Two shots were to be taken, one in right profile and the other in full face, and always in the same light and from the same angle and distance. He even had a special chair constructed. That way, each criminal would be photographed in the same position. And grinning or distorting the features was strictly forbidden.

From these clear, standardized photographs, Bertillon cut out hundreds of eyes, noses, mouths, and ears. He pasted them in long rows on strips of paper and studied them for hours on end. He was looking for certain types of features that could be described in precise language. A nose, for example, could have a flattened bridge, a crushed bridge, a narrow bridge, or a wide bridge. Bertillon also spent hour after hour looking into prisoners' eyes to find words to describe the dozens of subtle gradations of color.

Bertillon then reduced each descriptive word or phrase to a letter code. Strung together, these letters made up a formula unique to each criminal. This formula, the eleven measurements, and the two photographs all were pasted onto a single index card. The result was what Bertillon called a *portrait parlé*—a picture that speaks.

As time passed, Bertillon's fame grew. Visitors from all over Europe came to watch him measure and photo-

taille 1⁼ 78.0	⎰ long⁹ 19.4	pied g. 27.4	⎰ n° de cl. 3	âge de 48
voûte ⟋	tête ⎱ larg⁹ 16.8	médius g. 11.9	Coul⁹ de l'iris ⎰ aur⁹ ʀ.oʀ.ɪɪɪ	né le 22-4 18 53
envᵉʳg. 1⁼ 81	⎰ bi-zyg⁹ 14.7	auricᵉˢ g. 9.9	⎱ pér⁹ᵉ aʀ.ᴅ.ᴠ.ɪɪɪ	à Paris
buste 0⁼ 95.2	oreille dr. 6.7	coudée g. 47.9	⎱ part⁹ᵉ	dép⁹ 1ᵛᵉ âge appᵗ ⸗

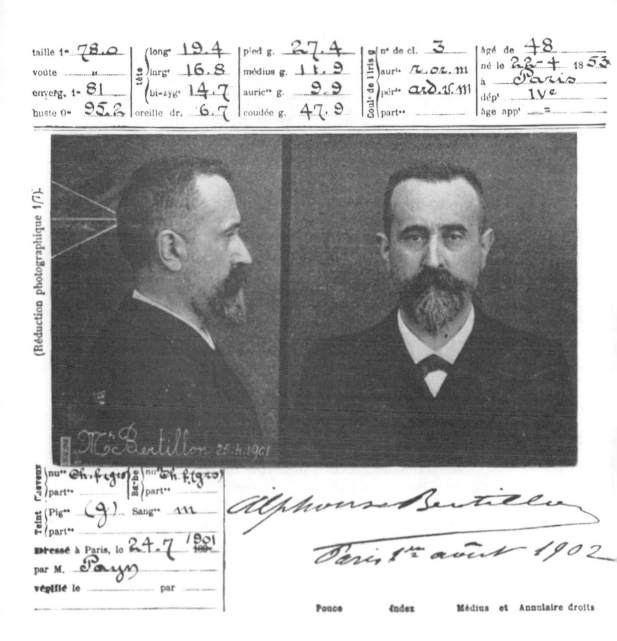

(Réduction photographique 1/7).

Mⁿᵉ Bertillon 25.4.1901

| Cheveux ⎰ nu⁹ᵉ Ch.f.(gʳˢ) | Barbe ⎰ nu⁹ᵉ Ch.f.(gʳˢ) |
| ⎱ part⁹ᵉ | ⎱ part⁹ᵉ |
| Teint ⎰ Pig⁹ᵉ (g) Sang⁹ᵉ ɪɪɪ |
| ⎱ part⁹ᵉ |

Dressé à Paris, le 24.7 1901

par M. Payn

vérifié le ____ par ____

Alphonse Bertillon

Paris 1ᵉʳ août 1902

Pouce   Index   Médius et Annulaire droits

Bertillon's own portrait parlé

graph criminals. By 1888, his archive of portraits parlé had grown to nearly half a million separate descriptions. Bertillon's title was now Director of the Police Identification Service. On February 1, he moved his operations to new, roomier quarters in the attic of the courthouse. The floorboards were rotting and flakes of plaster fluttered from the ceiling, but Bertillon was grateful to have a workplace of his own at last.

Four years later, on March 11, 1892, a case arose that lifted Bertillon's fame to new heights. It began explosively, with the bombing of a house in Paris. At first, authorities thought it was a gas explosion. Then, amid the rubble on the second floor, the remains of a bomb were discovered. The address was Number 136 Boulevard Saint-Germain—the home of Presiding Judge Benoit.

In May 1891, Benoit had presided over the trial of a band of anarchists. At that time, *anarchy* was an unsettling political and social movement. It called for the end of all forms of government and law. Anarchists were prepared to use any means necessary, including terrorism, to cause disorder and stir up revolt anywhere and everywhere they could.

Politicians and judges were the anarchists' prime targets. They had already made attempts on the lives of the king of Spain, the king of Italy, and Kaiser Wilhelm I of Germany. Many people believed that the anarchists had planted the bomb that exploded in Judge Benoit's home. They wondered where the terrorists would strike next.

They didn't have to wait long for an answer. On Sunday, March 27, a bomb exploded at Number 39 Rue de Clichy—the home of State Prosecutor General Bulot. Outraged citizens throughout Paris demanded that the police capture and prosecute the bomber.

Some evidence suggested that an anarchist named Ravachol might be responsible. The police wanted to find him and bring him in for questioning. So far, however, they had been unable to find Ravachol.

Bertillon was called in on the case by a police force desperate for success. Three years earlier, Ravachol had been arrested for theft and brought to Bertillon for measurement. He'd called himself Koenigstein then, an alias known to the police. Bertillon quickly located the Koenigstein description in the archive. Included in the portrait parlé was the fact that the man had a scar on his left hand, near the thumb.

A full description of the suspect, drawn from Bertillon's portrait parlé, was published in Paris newspapers. A few days later, a restaurant owner on the Boulevard Magenta sent an urgent message to the police. A man matching Ravachol's description—5 feet 4 inches (163 cm) tall with a pale complexion, dark beard, and a scar near the thumb of the left hand—was having breakfast at his cafe.

Police rushed to the restaurant and captured Ravachol, but not without a fierce struggle. Still bloody from the battle, Ravachol was brought to Bertillon, who took Ravachol's measurements and checked them against the index card bearing Koenigstein's description. They matched exactly. Ravachol was found guilty and condemned to death. His last words, as the blade of the *guillotine* fell, were: "You pigs, long live the Revolution!"[3]

Bertillon's identification of Ravachol got sensational headlines in France and all over Europe. One journalist wrote: "Bertillonage, based upon the measurements of certain unchanging parts of the skeleton, is the greatest and most brilliant invention the nineteenth century has produced in the field of criminology. Long live bertillonage! Long live Alphonse Bertillon!"[4]

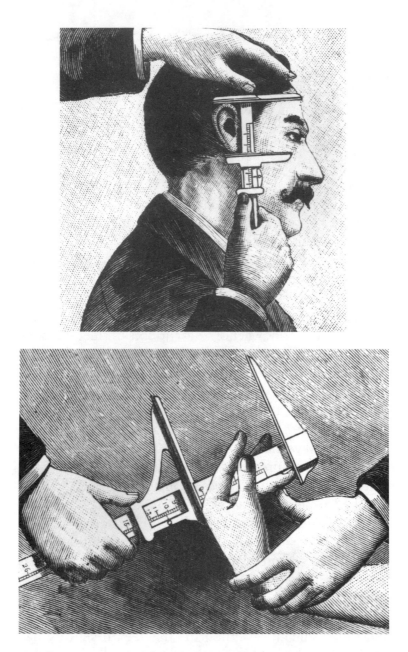

Bertillon's intricate identification system relied on precise measurements.

Suddenly, bertillonage was on the minds of police officials everywhere. It was introduced in the United States in 1887 by Major Robert McClaughry, warden of the Illinois State Penitentiary at Joliet. Most police forces outside Europe were still reluctant to adopt it, however.

The problem was the system's complexity. Complaints came in from police officials and detectives far and wide. Bertillonage was too complicated, they said. There were too many formulas and codes to memorize. And taking accurate measurements demanded precision. If one measurement was incorrect, the whole portrait parlé could be thrown out of whack. Bertillon's system was simply too difficult for the average police officer to master. Still, bertillonage was acknowledged by most police officials and members of the scientific community as the best method in existence for identifying and keeping track of criminals.

A year after the Ravachol affair, Scotland Yard, the police headquarters in London, sent a committee to Paris to meet with Bertillon and watch him in action. Known as the Troup Committee, they were impressed with much of what they saw, especially Bertillon's revolutionary techniques in crime-scene photography. Bertillon had devised a metric grid that attached to the camera lens. This meant that the scene was photographed in measured sections, each of which could then be analyzed separately.

But they were not nearly as impressed with bertillonage. "Bertillon's work is perhaps more of a theoretical than of a practical nature," the committee declared.[5]

Besides, the British were now equally interested in using another new scientific system of criminal identification—a British system. Although this new British system was largely untested and unrefined, it seemed to promise all the benefits of bertillonage without any of the drawbacks.

Bertillon came to know this new system only too well. Eventually, he reluctantly began to use it himself to solve several famous cases. However, this proud, determined man, the father of forensic science, would always fight a fierce battle to keep this British system, known as *fingerprinting*, from making his precious bertillonage a thing of the past.

CHAPTER 2
"FOR THE PURPOSE OF FIXING IDENTITY"

Edward Henry and the Landscape of the Fingertip

A tall thin man with a thick, dark mustache quickly plucked a pencil from his pocket. Edward Henry had just been struck by a lightning bolt of inspiration.

Inspirations have a way of arriving when least expected. Henry looked all around the train car for something—anything—to write on. With no paper in sight, he was forced to sketch out his inspired thoughts on his starched white cuffs and shirtsleeves.

Meanwhile, the train chugged along through the Indian countryside. The year was 1896, and India was part of the British Empire. Edward Henry, a British police official, was crossing the Province of Bengal on his way to Calcutta.

Henry had been thinking about fingerprints, the raised ridges of skin that run in patterns of curving lines on the tips of our fingers and thumbs. Under a magnifying glass these patterns can be seen clearly. What can't be seen are the tiny *pores* scattered along these ridges. These pores discharge oily perspiration from the sweat glands. This oily perspiration is what leaves fingerprints on just about anything a person touches.

Each fingerprint that's left behind is unique. It is also unchangeable. People with a desperate need to hide their identity have taken extreme measures to change their fingerprints. They've scrubbed their fingertips with sandpaper. They've burned them with acid. They've even peeled the skin away. But when the wounds healed and new skin grew back, the same patterns reappeared. They had the exact same fingerprints as before.

Fingerprints have fascinated people for thousands of years. But no one had discovered a system for classifying

Distinctively curved patterns of ridges and pores form this one-of-a-kind fingerprint.

them until Edward Henry had his lightning bolt of inspiration in 1896. It didn't take long for Henry to cover the long sleeves of his white shirt with formulas. These formulas could be applied to the fingerprints of anyone on earth, and they would positively identify that person as unique from everyone else—past, present, and future.

Henry had no idea of the staggering importance of the system he was creating. If he could have climbed out

Englishman Edward Henry had help in developing his revolutionary system for identifying fingerprints.

of that train car into a time machine and shot ahead to the beginning of the twenty-first century, he would have seen that his system for classifying fingerprints was being used in hospitals, government agencies, and police departments all around the world. He would have learned that his formulas had been used to bring countless criminals to justice as well as to identify missing persons and the casualties of war.

It would be inaccurate to say that Edward Henry was acting alone as he developed a system for classifying fingerprints. His momentous idea would not have been possible without the efforts of other pioneering scientists who came before him.

One of these pioneers was Francis Galton. Henry knew that Galton also had been working on a system for classifying fingerprints. Two years earlier, while home in England on vacation, Henry had visited Galton's laboratory.

Like most scientists of the late nineteenth century, Francis Galton thought science could explain everything. He believed the key to understanding something lay in measuring and classifying its component parts. Galton's passion for measurement had led him to design a special tool for measuring the wingspan of a moth. He had also attempted to measure precisely the beauty of a woman and the power of prayer.

Like Alphonse Bertillon, Francis Galton was fascinated with the landscape of the human body. He was especially drawn to tiny surface details, such as the markings in the iris of the eye and the size and shape of the ear. But of all these markings, it was fingerprints that fascinated Galton most.

"Perhaps the most beautiful and characteristic of all superficial marks," Galton wrote, "are the small furrows with the intervening ridges and their pores that are dis-

Francis Galton's fascination with fingerprints helped Edward Henry develop his identification system.

posed in a singularly complex yet even order on the undersurfaces of the hands."[1]

This fascination blossomed in 1888, when Galton was asked to give a lecture to members of the Royal Institute of London. The subject was bertillonage. Galton had paid a visit to Bertillon in Paris, and Bertillon's system for identifying criminals had impressed him. But Galton also observed how overly complicated and prone to error that system could be.

Wasn't there a better way of identifying criminals? What about fingerprinting?

Galton had read two articles on fingerprints in *Nature*, a popular British science magazine. One of the authors was Dr. Henry Faulds, a Scottish physician and surgeon living in Japan. "The Chinese criminals from early times have been made to give the impressions of their finger, just as we make ours yield their photographs," Faulds wrote. "The Egyptians caused their criminals to seal their confessions with their thumb nails, just as the Japanese do now."[2] Faulds also noted that the Japanese had signed legal documents of all sorts with thumbprints and handprints.

This was all very interesting to Galton. But it was something else Faulds wrote that had stuck in his mind through the years: "When bloody finger marks or impressions on clay, glass, etc., exist, they may lead to the scientific identification of criminals."[3]

This was a revolutionary idea. Faulds was the first European to suggest using fingerprints to help catch and convict lawbreakers. And what's more, Faulds had actually done this himself. A house in Faulds's Tokyo neighborhood was robbed, and the thief left his fingerprints on a teacup. Luckily, over the years, Faulds had built up a collection of fingerprints of people in his neighborhood.

Looking through his collection, Faulds spotted a print that matched the one on the teacup.

It belonged to a servant in a nearby household. When the police confronted the servant with the evidence, he confessed. Thus, Dr. Henry Faulds became the first person to solve a crime by using fingerprints found at the scene.

Faulds had also used fingerprints to save an innocent man from jail. During another burglary, the thief left his sooty fingerprints on a whitewashed wall. When Faulds heard that the police had a suspect in custody, he took the man's fingerprints. They were different from the thief's sooty fingerprints, and Faulds convinced the police that they had the wrong man.

A few days later, another man was arrested. When Faulds found that this second suspect's fingerprints matched the sooty set on the whitewashed wall, the police knew that they had the right man.

Solving these crimes convinced Faulds that he was onto something important. "There can be no doubt as to the advantage of having, beside their photographs, a nature copy of the forever unchangeable finger-furrows of important criminals," he wrote.[4]

A reader responded to Faulds's *Nature* magazine article with a bitter letter, which the magazine also published. William Herschel was the writer. The way Herschel saw it, Faulds was trying to take credit for Herschel's ideas.

William Herschel had been working with fingerprints for two decades. Like Edward Henry, he was a British civil servant stationed in India. As chief administrative officer of a district of Bengal Province, Herschel was in charge of issuing pension checks to retired Indian soldiers.

Before Herschel took over, many of these pension checks had been claimed by impostors—other people posing as the soldiers. These swindlers could get away with their crimes because most of the soldiers were illiterate and couldn't sign their names to positively prove their identity.

Herschel ended the swindling once and for all with one simple rule. Every man who came to collect a check must press his right hand on an ink pad and then "sign" a piece of paper with his handprint. If his handprint didn't match, he didn't get a check and he might end up in jail.

As years passed, Herschel noticed something fascinating. Over time, the soldiers' outward appearances changed. They lost weight or gained it, their faces became wrinkled, and their hair turned gray. But their fingerprints never changed.

With this in mind, Herschel began fingerprinting convicted criminals and keeping the results on file. It was no longer possible for former convicts to tell a judge that they'd never been imprisoned before. It was also impossible for criminals to pay someone else to impersonate them and serve their sentence in jail.

Herschel read Faulds's *Nature* article with dismay. Herschel saw it as an attempt to take credit for ideas that that he, not Faulds, should be given credit for. But in his bitter letter to *Nature*, Herschel ignored the fact that Faulds had come up with a truly original idea: using fingerprints found at the scene of the crime to catch criminals.

After Faulds's article and Herschel's letter were published, neither man did anything more to advance the science of fingerprinting. Neither man took the next logical step: to devise a simple classification system for keeping track of fingerprints.

But their work was not wasted. Their articles published in *Nature* intrigued Francis Galton. He decided to devise a system for classifying fingerprints. Galton informed William Herschel of his intentions in a letter. Herschel responded by sending Galton all his material on fingerprinting, in the hope that his work might be put to some practical use at last.

Included in Herschel's material were impressions that he had taken of his own fingerprints. He'd taken them periodically, from 1860 to 1888. Galton examined them closely. Yes, they did seem to prove that a person's fingerprints remain unchanged throughout his lifetime. But Galton had to see for himself, so he began assembling his own collection. Just as Bertillon's father and grandfather had measured their Paris visitors, Galton took the fingerprints of everyone who visited his London laboratory.

Galton immediately saw that fingerprinting took much less time and effort than anthropometry. The procedure he used, known as ink and roll, was quick and simple. All he needed was a stamp pad and a piece of white paper. One by one, he rolled the fingertips on the inked pad, from one side of the nail to the other. Then he rolled the inked fingertips on the paper. The black ink from the raised ridges and the white space in the furrows between them left the unique pattern.

Within 3 years, Galton had collected more fingerprints than Herschel. After examining his collection, Galton drew these conclusions:

- Each person has ten different fingerprints.

- Fingerprints never change during a person's lifetime.

- Each fingerprint is unique.

- The possibility of two people having the same fingerprints is 64 billion to 1.

Galton included these conclusions in his textbook *Fingerprints*, published in 1892. Using Faulds and Herschel's work, Galton had taken the science of fingerprinting to the next level. He was the first to systematically analyze fingerprints and to propose a system for classifying them.

Galton's classification system was based on three basic patterns, which he named arches, loops, and *whorls*. On the basis of his book and Scotland Yard's Troup Committee report (see Chapter 1), Galton convinced the British government to use fingerprinting as a supplement to bertillonage.

But by his own estimates, Galton was years away from developing his system to the point where it would be truly useful in identifying criminals. Police departments all across Europe still relied on Bertillon's system of identification.

Gradually, Galton lost interest in fingerprinting and moved on to other pursuits. Meanwhile, Edward Henry became interested in fingerprints. He was familiar with the ideas of Galton, Herschel, and Faulds. He kept thinking about fingerprinting whenever he had a chance. Then, one day, everything fell into place. As you know, the lightning bolt of inspiration came as Henry was on a train to Calcutta. What exactly did Henry write all over the cuffs and sleeves of his shirt?

The scientific method involves breaking large problems down into smaller ones. That was what Henry had done that day. He'd found a way of breaking Galton's groupings into smaller subgroupings. He began by classifying ridges and furrows into five separate patterns instead of the three—arches, loops and whorls—used by Galton. Henry's patterns included:

- plain arches—rounded at the top,

- tented arches—pointed,

- radial loops—running toward the thumb,

- ulnar loops—running toward the little finger,

- whorls—circular.

Henry then broke each of these five patterns into subpatterns based on smaller variations, known as ridge characteristics or *minutiae*. They include forks, dots, islands, hooks, and bridges. The type, number, and position of these characteristics make each fingerprint unique—and classifiable.

In Henry's system, these characteristics are represented by letters and numbers which, when joined together, make a formula. Henry's formulas were similar to the ones Bertillon used in his portrait parlé. But unlike bertillonage, Henry's fingerprinting system was easy to learn and use. And the results never varied.

"If this registration procedure proves reliable, I think it likely that anthropometry [bertillonage] will gradually be abandoned," Henry wrote.[5] Henry was right, but it did not happen for many years. Bertillon had worked long and hard before his identification system was accepted. Henry would face a similar struggle. And just like Bertillon, Henry would need some luck. His first stroke of good fortune came in 1898.

To take advantage of good fortune, you have to be ready for it. By 1898, Henry's fingerprinting system was fully operational in India. Tens of thousands of sets of criminals' fingerprints were on file.

In August of that year, in a remote area of Bengal, the manager of a tea plantation was found dead. His throat had been brutally slashed. Here was where the luck came in: The murderer had left a fingerprint on a card in the manager's wallet.

The card was sent to Henry in Calcutta. He also asked for the fingerprints of the dead man and all the plantation employees. When he found that none of these prints matched the prints on the manager's card, Henry turned to his files—the prints he had systematically built up over many years

Henry's years of work paid off—he found a perfect match. The matching fingerprints belonged to a man named Charan. He was a former servant on the plantation. His fingerprints were on file because he had been found guilty of theft 2 years earlier. Charan was soon tracked down, convicted, and sentenced—all thanks to Edward Henry's fingerprinting system.

The Charan Affair, as it became known in the popular press, inspired Edward Henry to keep refining his system. (He would eventually identify 1,024 separate fingerprint characteristics.) News of the Charan Affair eventually made its way back to London. People became increasingly interested in Henry's book, *Classification and Uses of Fingerprints*.

Not long after that, Henry was asked to come to London. In March 1901, he was appointed Acting Police Commissioner and head of the Criminal Investigation Department of New Scotland Yard. Henry used his authority to create the Central Fingerprint Bureau. He hired and trained the staff.

Even with his fingerprinting system firmly in place, Henry still had a great deal to prove. Judges and juries all over Great Britain and Europe had little or no experience with fingerprints as evidence. And many police officials

This magazine caricature of Edward Henry appropriately emphasizes his fingertips.

still thought bertillonage was the system they should be using.

Some of them changed their minds, though, when they heard about the Fox twins. Ebenezer Albert Fox and Albert Ebenezer Fox were identical twins. They were also wanted for poaching—illegally hunting and fishing on private property. For years, Ebenezer Albert and Albert Ebenezer had been getting away with their crimes because police could never be sure which twin was which. Bertillonage was no help: The twins' appearances and measurements were virtually identical.

Henry ended the Fox twins' poaching spree by taking their fingerprints. From then on, police had no trouble proving which twin was which.

The London police welcomed fingerprinting. They needed all the help they could get in identifying and catching criminals. At that time, anyone walking city streets at night ran the risk of being robbed. Electricity and motorcars were not yet widely available. The gas-lit streets and alleys of London were cloaked in flickering shadows, and the police had no rapid transport—only horses and carts. Also, very few people had telephones, so communication was not nearly as swift and efficient as it is today. And while criminals were free to arm themselves with guns and knives, the London police could carry nothing more lethal than clubs.

During its first year in use, the Henry system yielded impressive results. Three times more people were identified by fingerprinting than by bertillonage. "Fingerprints are better than a confession," Henry wrote. "A confession can be retracted, fingerprints can't."[6]

Due to newspaper articles about the Fox twins and other successful uses of fingerprinting, the technique was becoming more and more familiar to people outside of law enforcement. The popular American author Mark

This London policeman stands steadfastly in the flickering glow of a gas streetlight.

Twain also helped acquaint the public with fingerprinting. In his 1894 mystery novel *Pudd'nhead Wilson*, fingerprints provide evidence that dramatically saves two innocent men from the gallows.

Nevertheless, people remained skeptical. "The day hasn't dawned when a British court will accept fingerprints as conclusive evidence of identity," Henry wrote.[7] Most people had trouble believing that no two people on Earth have the same fingerprints. The idea seemed too fantastic to be true. Henry knew that it would take a series of popular successes to overcome judges' and juries' natural resistance to this highly technical new method of identification.

One early dramatic success came in 1904. It was an ordinary burglary—with one extraordinary detail. A burglar broke into a warehouse in the Clerkenwell district of London. Although he escaped, he left something highly personal behind. While scurrying over a high fence, the burglar took tight hold of one of the narrow iron spikes that ran along the top. He was wearing a ring on his little finger. As he vaulted over the top, the ring caught on the pointed tip of a spike. While the burglar was able to jump down and escape, his bloody finger remained at the scene of the crime.

An alert policeman spotted the incriminating digit— bloody and dangling from the spike—and had it sent to New Scotland Yard for examination. After police wiped it clean of blood, they took a fingerprint. It matched a fingerprint the Yard had on file. The burglar—minus the telltale finger—was soon in custody.

Henry's big break came a year later. On the morning of March 27, 1905, a storeowner and his wife were found murdered in their paint store. Their skulls had been brutally crushed. The store's cashbox was empty, showing that the murderer's motive was robbery. Chief Inspector Fox had the cashbox taken to Scotland Yard and checked for *latent* fingerprints.

Modern methods of developing latent fingerprints include the use of laser light and chemical vapors. Henry's men did not have these sophisticated techniques available to them. Instead, they used a fine graphite powder applied with a soft-haired brush. The powder was ap-

LATENT FINGERPRINTS

"Latent" means nearly invisible, or hidden. Some fingerprints, such as the ones Faulds's sooty-fingered thief left on the whitewashed wall, are plainly visible. But most are of the latent variety. Even though latent fingerprints are all but invisible, they are nearly permanent if they are left undisturbed on a hard surface. Latent fingerprints thousands of years old have been discovered in ancient tombs. But these nearly invisible marks must be developed, just as a photograph is developed, before they can be analyzed and identified.

plied carefully and lightly until the pattern became visible on the box's black enamel surface.

The print was smudged and blurry, but it had, as Henry put it, "sufficient clearly defined characteristic detail for the purpose of fixing identity."[8] The developed fingerprint was then photographed to obtain a permanent image. This image was then compared with the fingerprints of the victims. It didn't match. Next, it was compared to the thousands of fingerprints the Yard had on record. It didn't match any of them. The murderer had never been arrested before.

The police began to search Deptford—the London neighborhood where the crime had occurred—for the person who had left that unidentified fingerprint at the scene of the crime. Henry's men interviewed dozens of people, and kept their eyes and ears open.

Their methodical hunt paid off when a detective noticed a woman with a black eye in a pub—a neighborhood bar. He asked how she got the black eye. She told the police officer that a man named Albert Stratton was responsible. The officer asked her a few more questions and learned that Albert had a brother named Alfred. The men had been out on the night of the murder, but the woman wasn't sure where.

The police tracked down the Stratton brothers and brought them in for questioning. When Henry's men took their fingerprints, the brothers laughed and said it tickled. No, they didn't commit the murders, they said. And no, they had no alibi. But they didn't need one, they insisted, because the police had no evidence against them.

But after examining their fingerprints, the officer in charge, Sergeant Collins, said, "I have found that the mark on the cashbox is in exact correspondence with the print of the right thumb of the elder prisoner [Alfred]."[9]

When the news reached Henry, he immediately put in a call to Richard Muir, the government's top prosecutor. With two such brutal murders, this was going to be a high profile case. Henry wanted to make sure the criminals were brought to justice and that the public knew a fingerprint was the key piece of evidence.

But was the evidence too slim? Would a judge and jury accept a single fingerprint as proof positive when fingerprinting was still so technical and untested?

Henry knew the government's case would have to be brilliantly presented to bring in a guilty verdict, so he chose Richard Muir to prosecute. A relentless worker, Muir never slept more than 5 hours a night. He methodically wrote all the relevant facts of his cases on index cards with colored pencils. When he tried the case, he constantly referred to these cards. He often shuffled and fanned them while he was in the court room. "There's Muir at his card game," people would say.[10]

Muir too realized that he had a delicate case on his hands. More than the Stratton brothers would be judged here. Fingerprinting itself would be on trial. As he presented his case against the Stratton brothers, Muir would have to educate the judge and jury about fingerprints.

To make matters even more difficult, the defense had called in their own fingerprint expert to advise them. Their expert was Dr. Henry Faulds—the first man to catch a criminal using fingerprints found at the scene of the crime.

Since his days in Tokyo, Faulds had moved back to England and was now a police physician. Before Edward Henry took over at New Scotland Yard, Faulds had tried to get the police in both England and France interested in using fingerprints to solve crimes. He'd even offered to test his ideas for them at his own expense. But they had turned him down. Since Faulds had no classification system to offer, the French and English police had elected to stay with bertillonage—until Edward Henry came along.

For years now, Faulds had been writing letters and pamphlets claiming that he, Dr. Henry Faulds—not Edward Henry or Francis Galton or William Herschel—deserved the credit for discovering fingerprints as a tool for catching criminals. These men had conspired to keep him from the fame and fortune he deserved, Faulds believed. And here, apparently, was his chance to get even.

The prosecution presented its case against the brothers. "There is not the shadow of a doubt that the thumbprint on this money-box comes from the right thumb of the defendant Alfred Stratton," Muir told the judge and jury.[11]

Then Muir called Sergeant Collins of Scotland Yard to testify. On a chalkboard behind Collins, enlarged photos of two thumbprints were on display. One was from the cashbox and the other was from Alfred Stratton's thumb. Together, Muir and Collins showed the judge and jury how the two thumbprints matched exactly. They concluded by saying that only one person on earth could possibly have made these two thumbprints, and that was the accused—Alfred Stratton.

The Strattons' attorneys did their best to demolish the government's case against their clients. They used a strategy designed by Faulds. They too compared the two thumbprints on the chalkboard. But instead of pointing out the similarities, they pointed out all the little differences. Wasn't this ridge on Print A thicker than the corresponding ridge on Print B? And weren't these ridges on Print B darker than the corresponding ridges on Print A? They continued to do this until the jury's faith in Edward Henry's system had been severely tested, if not shaken.

Then it was Muir and Collins's turn. They knew exactly why these little differences existed. Now, if they could just convince the jury. Muir knew that a picture could be worth a thousand words. He also knew the power of dramatic courtroom demonstrations, and this seemed like a good place for one. So, rather than telling the jury that the Strattons' lawyers were misleading them, he showed them.

Muir had Collins take the thumbprints of the people on the jury. That way they could feel for themselves how difficult it was to always roll the fingers over the paper with the same amount of pressure. They could also see that the harder their thumb was pressed onto the paper, the thicker and darker the resulting print appeared.

Only after completing this demonstration did Muir explain what the jury had just seen and felt for themselves. The differences between the fingerprints were the result of pressure exerted on the paper. But the patterns—from the 1,024 separate characteristics in Edward Henry's system—did not vary.

By now it was painfully clear to the Strattons' lawyers that their expert's advice had been anything but expert. They realized, too late, that Faulds had acted out of resentment toward Edward Henry—a resentment that had blinded him to the truth.

In his instructions to the jury, a cautious Judge Channell said, "There is an extraordinary amount of resemblance between the two marks we have seen, and therefore they are, to a certain extent, corroborative evidence in regard to Alfred Stratton, but I do not think you, gentlemen of the jury, would wish to act upon these marks alone."[12]

So, a thread of hope remained for the Strattons. However, it was soon broken. The jury found both brothers guilty as charged, and the judge condemned them to death by hanging. This marked the first time a British court had convicted suspects of murder based on fingerprint evidence, and it gave Edward Henry's fingerprinting system instant credibility.

One by one, country after country began adopting Henry's system and phasing out bertillonage: Hungary, Austria, Germany, Spain, Switzerland, Denmark, and the United States. Finally, even France—Bertillon's own country—abandoned bertillonage.

It is only natural that Bertillon's system was eventually surpassed by a new system. After all, that's how science works. Scientific knowledge is always growing and changing, so one new discovery often leads to several others.

Unfortunately, Bertillon was not prepared for this natural course of events. The father of forensic science witnessed the death of his pioneering system of criminal identification with the stubborn defiance that had characterized his entire life. He continued to disdainfully refer to fingerprints as "those tiny spots on human fingertips."

He insisted that "skin markings have insufficiently distinct gradations to serve as a basis for identification."[13] But the Deptford case—and the thousands upon thousands of cases that followed over the years—proved Bertillon wrong.

Meanwhile, in another part of Europe, an entirely different system of criminal identification was being developed. Unlike bertillonage and fingerprinting, this new system would go beneath the skin—where the stuff of life flows.

CHAPTER 3
"AN ABSURD DREAM"
Karl Landsteiner and
the Mysteries of Blood

In 1901, an Austrian physiologist named Karl Landsteiner published a scientific paper that would eventually catapult the field of forensic science forward. Just as Edward Henry had learned the secret code of fingerprints, Landsteiner was coming to understand the mysterious code that distinguishes one type of human blood from another.

Unlike Henry, however, Landsteiner was a shy man. He was an extremely talented scientist, but he wasn't so successful at getting his message out to the world. In the early 1900s, Landsteiner's work was well known in Vienna—the city where he lived and worked—but it was almost unknown outside Austria. It wasn't until 1915 that forensic scientists in other countries began using Landsteiner's ideas to help catch criminals.

Before law-enforcement officials could see the value of Landsteiner's work, they needed to develop some more basic techniques. First of all, they needed a reliable method for proving that a stain was actually blood, and

Austrian Karl Landsteiner saw blood as a series of secrets to uncover.

not some other substance. They also needed a technique that could determine whether the blood was from a human, and not some other animal.

The first of these goals was achieved around the turn of the twentieth century. A new tool, called the *spectroscope*, made it possible to differentiate a bloodstain from other types of stains. A spectroscope produces a microscopic picture of the radiant energy patterns given off by a substance. These radiant energy patterns are as distinctive as fingerprints. Blood has its own characteristic pattern, and that pattern is different from the pattern of any other substance on earth.

The spectroscope was extremely useful, but it could not distinguish between the blood of a human and the blood of another animal. Cat blood, cow blood, and canary blood all produce the same spectroscopic image as human blood. This was a problem because, as far as the law was concerned, it was not enough to prove that a stain on a suspect's clothing was blood. Unless forensic scientists could prove that the blood was from a human, the evidence could not be used in court. After all, a suspect could claim the blood was from a slaughtered farm animal.

On February 7, 1901, Paul Uhlenhuth, an assistant professor at a small German university, announced that he had devised a reliable method for distinguishing human blood from the blood of other animals. Uhlenhuth had worked from a base of knowledge developed 5 years earlier by a Belgian scientist named Jules Bordet.

Bordet had discovered that blood from one animal *species* is not compatible with blood from another species. When blood taken from an animal of one species (the donor) was injected into an animal of another species (the receiver), the receiver's blood would *clot*—or form clumps. This meant that the receiver's blood was waging a war against the donor's blood.

Uhlenhuth took Bordet's discoveries a step further when he developed the *precipitin test*. This test used a *serum* developed from rabbit blood. Serum is the colorless liquid part of blood, minus the red and white blood *cells*. Serum contains the blood's *antibodies*—the "soldiers" that fight off disease. When these antibodies react with the invading blood cells, the blood clots.

Uhlenhuth's rabbit serum reacted with human blood only. It did not react with blood from other animals. When the rabbit serum was mixed with human blood, the blood cells clotted, and a whitish substance called a *precipitate* formed. But when this same rabbit serum was mixed with blood from other animals, no precipitate formed. Uhlenhuth's rabbit serum was the tool that forensic scientists had been dreaming of. It could determine whether a bloodstain was—or was not—made of human blood.

Police forces all across Europe hailed Uhlenhuth's precipitin test. When a suspect claimed that bloodstains on his clothes came from an animal, the precipitin test could prove him right or wrong.

There was still one problem, however. The suspect could claim that the stains were made by his own blood and not the victim's. He could say, "I had a nosebleed," knowing that the police still had no way to distinguish one person's blood from another person's blood. Uhlenhuth's precipitin test could prove only that the blood came from a human. It could not determine which human.

Most people thought it was impossible to distinguish between the blood of two people. According to one French criminologist, "Only a few persons of imagination looked forward to the next task: to demonstrate that a

German Paul Uhlenhuth discovered a foolproof way to distinguish human blood from the blood of other animals.

given bloodstain came not from a human being in general, but from a particular human being. The possibility seemed an absurd dream."[1]

This is where Karl Landsteiner comes into the story. At the time, he was looking for a way to make *blood transfusions* more successful. When injuries caused a patient to lose a lot of blood, the patient would die unless some of the blood could be replaced. The patient needed fresh blood from healthy people.

When a transfusion worked, a life was saved. The problem was that transfusions didn't always work. And when they didn't, the patient died. No one could predict when a transfusion would work and when it would prove fatal.

Landsteiner thought he understood why some transfusions failed. Like Uhlenhuth, he knew about Bordet's discoveries concerning serum, antibodies, and clotting. He hypothesized that different types of blood ran through people's veins, and that these different blood types were not all compatible. When two incompatible types of blood were mixed together, the blood would clot and the patient would die.

Landsteiner wondered if he could put all this knowledge together to develop a method for identifying blood types. More importantly, could he determine which blood types were compatible? Landsteiner knew that if he could accomplish these goals, doctors would be able to give safe transfusions all the time.

Landsteiner started to conduct experiments. Like Uhlenhuth, he worked with blood serums. To produce them, he used a *centrifuge*—a machine with a wheel of test tubes connected to a central axis that spins at high speeds. The liquids within the spinning test tubes are separated out into their various components. In this case, the liquids were blood samples, and the resulting components were serum and cells.

After centrifuging the samples, Landsteiner mixed red blood cells from one person's blood with serum from another person's blood. Depending on which samples of blood he used, one of two distinctly different reactions occurred. Either the serum and cells mixed peacefully with one another, or they reacted violently because antibodies attacked the invading cells. A violent reaction caused the blood to clot.

As you learned earlier, Landsteiner published these results in 1901. According to his scientific paper, "Blood serum of normal persons can frequently agglutinate [clot] the red blood corpuscles of other healthy individuals."[2] This *agglutination*, or clotting in the arteries and veins, was the cause of death from blood transfusions. It occurred because people have different types of blood. Some types of blood are compatible, but others are not. When incompatible blood types are mixed together, the blood clots. Since the patient's blood cannot flow, he or she dies.

Landsteiner had identified three different blood types. He called them Group A, Group B, and Group C. A year later, two of Landsteiner's assistants discovered a fourth blood group, which they called AB. Meanwhile, Group C had been renamed Group O. Modern scientists continue to recognize four major blood types—A, B, AB, and O.

Although Landsteiner was not thinking about forensic science when he performed his research, something he wrote in 1901 hinted strongly that blood typing could be useful in police work. "Agglutination [clotting] can also be produced with serum that has been dried, and then dissolved," he wrote. "It even succeeded with a

Karl Landsteiner was determined to learn why people were dying from blood transfusions.

solution made from a drop of blood dried on canvas, preserved for two weeks, and then dissolved."[3]

In other words, blood groups could be determined from dried bloodstains found on a criminal's skin or clothing. However, it wasn't until 1916 that a forensic scientist actually put Landsteiner's ideas to use.

Dr. Leone Lattes was a research assistant at the Institute of Forensic Medicine in Turin, Italy, at that time. One day a bloodstained coat was brought to him. It had been sent by a magistrate in Turin, who had heard of Lattes' research with dried bloodstains.

Lattes had successfully determined the blood type of tiny specks of blood up to 3 months old. Could he use the same process on bloodstains on the coat of Aldo Petrucci? Petrucci had been arrested for murder, but he insisted that he was innocent. Petrucci claimed the bloodstains did not belong to the murdered man. He said he often had nosebleeds, and claimed that the blood on his coat was his own.

The magistrate in Turin thought otherwise. Petrucci was a habitual criminal, and he had no alibi for the night of the crime. The 4-day-old bloodstains had been subjected to Uhlenhuth's precipitin test. The blood had definitely come from a human—but which human? The magistrate needed more information to convict Petrucci. Could Dr. Lattes help?

Lattes began by drawing a blood sample from the murdered man's heart. Then he went to Petrucci's jail cell and took a blood sample from the suspect. Next, Lattes placed a drop of solution made from the bloodstains on the coat onto two microscope slides. He then added a drop of fresh type A blood to one slide and a drop of fresh type B blood to the other slide. Lattes watched as the blood cells on both slides clumped together.

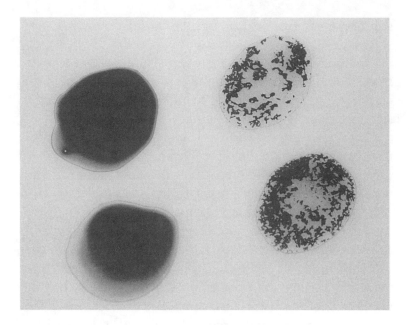

Blood compatibility tests show whether blood from one person can successfully be given to another. The circles of blood on the right of this photograph are clotting.

This told Lattes that the blood on Petrucci's coat came from a person with type O blood. Lattes' earlier tests had shown that the victim's blood was type A, and Petrucci's was type O. So, the bloodstains on the coat might well have come from Petrucci himself, as Petrucci claimed, but they could not possibly have come from the victim. If Petrucci had anything to do with the murder, the bloodstains on his coat did not prove it. The police had no other evidence against Petrucci, so he was released.

Lattes had a detailed account of his success on the Petrucci case circulated among police officials and other forensic scientists, but no one took any real interest, Seven years passed before Lattes worked on another criminal case.

This long delay was partly due to historical circumstances. World War I (1914–1918) was being fought in Europe. During that time, research not directly related to the war effort was halted.

But work with blood transfusions continued. Thanks to Karl Landsteiner's pioneering research, blood transfusions were no longer a deadly gamble. With all the battlefield injuries in this bloody war, blood transfusions were badly needed. They saved thousands of lives.

Lattes' second criminal case came along in 1923. By then, he had refined his blood-typing techniques. Now he could type bloodstains up to 18 months old. During the next few years, Lattes provided important evidence for several criminal cases. In 1925, he published an article that summed up the advantages and disadvantages of using blood typing in criminal cases.

The technique had one major disadvantage. It was still impossible to state with certainty that a bloodstain came from one particular person because each of the four blood types is shared by a great many people. In the United States, for instance, 45 percent of the population has type O blood, 42 percent has type A blood, 10 percent has type B blood, and 3 percent has type AB blood.

Yet, determining blood types did help narrow the list of suspects in violent crimes. If the bloodstains on a suspect's clothing did not match the victim's blood type, that suspect could be ruled out.

Blood-type evidence also put suspects under a great deal of pressure. Although blood-type evidence alone was not enough to convict, it could be quite persuasive. If a suspect could not explain the source of bloodstains that matched the victim's blood type, he came under heavy suspicion. In a number of cases like this, suspects broke down and confessed.

By 1926, a great many scientists had heard of Lattes and Landsteiner's work with blood typing. These scientists urged police departments in their communities to use the technique. Soon most police officials began to see the benefits of blood typing.

Recognition of Lattes and Landsteiner's achievements had been a long time in coming. A speaker at a meeting of forensic scientists in Berlin, Germany, summed it up: "Today, 25 years after the discovery of blood groups, the German Society for Forensic Medicine is discussing the Landsteiner reaction for what is probably the first time."[4]

But it was not the last time. Four years later, in 1930, Karl Landsteiner was awarded the Nobel Prize for his work with blood typing, dating back to 1901.

Landsteiner continued his work with blood typing. In 1933, he and his associates found that the existing four blood groups could be subdivided into six additional groups (A1, A2, M, N, MN, and P). When Landsteiner died in 1943, other scientists picked up where he left off. They continued his relentless search for even more blood groups. Today scientists recognize that the four major groups can be subdivided into about 300 groups. And, since Landsteiner's incredible discovery in 1901, countless violent criminals have been brought to justice by the tiniest trace of blood.

CHAPTER 4

"EVERY CONTACT LEAVES A TRACE"

Edmond Locard and the Microscope as Detective

In 1911, *counterfeit* coins were becoming a problem in Lyons, France. The police believed they knew who the culprits were, but they had no evidence against the men. When a forensic scientist named Edmond Locard was assigned to the case, he asked to examine the clothing of the three suspects.

The inspector in charge reluctantly granted Locard permission to examine the clothing of one suspect. The inspector could not imagine how a man's shirt and pants could prove that he was making counterfeit coins, but Locard knew exactly what he was doing.

In his examination of the man's clothing, Locard used a pair of tweezers to remove every last speck of dust from the pants pockets. He then carefully brushed every single speck of dust from the shirtsleeves onto sheets of white paper.

Using a microscope, Locard examined each and every speck of the collected dust. According to Locard, dust "contains distinctive characteristics which permit us to determine its origin."[1] If the men were making counterfeit metal coins, then traces of the metals might show up on their clothing.

Locard found what he was looking for—particles that seemed to be traces of metal. Chemical tests proved him right. The dust contained tin, antimony, and lead. Amazingly, the metals were present in the same proportions in the dust and in the counterfeit coins. Locard's examination of the other two men's clothing turned up similar results.

The three men were arrested. A few days later, the French newspapers announced that the men had confessed. This was just the kind of high-profile case that Locard had been longing for. For years, he had been working persistently with the hope that one day his efforts would be recognized.

In his work, Locard made use of basic principles he'd learned years earlier from Alexandre Lacassagne, a professor of *pathology* at the Institute of Forensic Medicine. Like Alphonse Bertillon, Edward Henry, and Karl Landsteiner, Lacassagne tried to find new and better methods of identifying people. Lacassagne was known for going to extremes in his work. He had once gone so far as to burn his fingertips with acid to prove to himself that it was impossible to alter fingerprints.

Lacassagne had become well known in 1889 when the Lyons police asked him to help identify a corpse. The victim had been stuffed into a wooden trunk and put on a train that ran from Paris to Lyons. The police had no idea who the victim was, what had caused his death, or why he had been stuffed into a trunk and put on a train.

When the police asked Lacassagne if he could discover the identity of the corpse, he seized the opportunity. He had recently developed new techniques for identifying human remains, and this was his chance to use these new methods.

64

Lacassagne's techniques worked. By examining the hair, bones, and teeth of the dead man, he was able to assemble enough information to identify the person as a Parisian court official named Gouffé. Lacassagne also managed to establish the cause of death—strangulation. The information collected by Lacassagne enabled the Paris police to apprehend Gouffé's killer. Eventually, the murderer lost his head to the guillotine.

Professor Alexandre Lacassagne taught Edmond Locard to look for the clues that police overlook.

Because the circumstances of the Gouffé Affair were so bizarre, the case was described in newspapers throughout France. This publicity made Lacassagne instantly famous. And his newfound fame brought him more students. One of those students was Locard.

Professors are sometimes on the lookout for that one special student who will carry their ideas to the next level. For Lacassagne, Locard was that special student. Edmond Locard used what he learned from Lacassagne and others to revolutionize forensic science.

Professor Alexandre Lacassagne encouraged his students to look at things from a logical, scientific point of view. "Keep your eyes open for all the little clues that the police overlook," he told them. Foremost among these overlooked clues was dust.

Lacassagne often quoted a German chemist named Leibing on the subject: "Dust contains in small all the things that surround us."[2] Lacassagne insisted that his students pay special attention to even the smallest bits of dust on clothing, in hair, on shoes, and underneath fingernails. He instructed them to methodically examine every possible piece of evidence. After all, the tiniest particles might hold vital secrets that only a trained, alert observer could detect.

Locard took these instructions to heart. He was also impressed by the German criminologist Hans Gross. Locard studied Gross's textbook, *Criminal Investigation*, which was published in 1893. In it, Gross advised police to use bertillonage in their work and to carefully examine crime scenes for traces of blood and fingerprints. Gross also promoted the use of the microscope in police work. Detectives who ignored the microscope would miss vital clues, he said. Hair, pollen, bits of thread, and dust could all be important evidence.

Gross also advised police to consult scientists of all sorts—chemists, mineralogists, botanists, zoologists, and even physicists. Clues, he explained, were to be found in the most unexpected ways and in the most unexpected places.

Like Lacassagne's instructions, Gross's ideas stayed with Locard. Later, he would use them all. He would also use the ideas of Arthur Conan Doyle, the English doctor and writer who created the popular fictional detective Sherlock Holmes. Locard had read the Holmes stories in French translation.

In Doyle's stories, Sherlock Holmes uses unusual methods that would not be used by real detectives until years later. It was as if Doyle could see into the future. In *A Study in Scarlet* (1887), for instance, Sherlock Holmes discovers a method for typing human blood—14 years before Karl Landsteiner made the actual discovery. Holmes relied on *trace evidence*, such as dust and ashes, 6 years before Hans Gross recommended the very same thing in his textbook.

Holmes took identification to extremes. He could distinguish among 140 different kinds of cigar, cigarette, and pipe tobacco ash. He could identify seventy-five kinds of perfume by their scent. He could identify people by their handwriting, and knew exactly which typewriter had been used to write a letter. He could tell the exact height of a man by examining his footprints.

These feats of deduction seemed all but impossible until Doyle had his fictional detective explain how he'd arrived at them. The explanations always made perfect sense. "Elementary," Holmes would say, as if these mental feats were simple to perform. And in a way, they were. But only if the detective looked at the facts carefully—from a logical, scientific point of view.

The Holmes stories inspired Locard. They were a vivid demonstration of what Lacassagne and Gross had said and written—that a scientific-minded person could see far more than an ordinary person. Locard was especially intrigued with Doyle's descriptions of Holmes's rooms at 221B Baker Street. The residence was cluttered with a scientific sleuth's tools of the trade—microscopes, test tubes, Bunsen burners, reference books, and more.

After reading Doyle's stories, Locard's vision took real shape. He wanted to create a place where all the tools of crime detection were brought together under one roof. This collection of tools would combine all the knowledge and techniques gathered by Bertillon, Henry, Landsteiner, Lacassagne, and Gross. Locard was envisioning the world's first crime laboratory.

To give life to his revolutionary vision, Locard would have to do some research. His crime laboratory would have all the latest and best tools of scientific crime detection. To find the best equipment and techniques, Locard took an important trip. First, he visited Bertillon in Paris. Then he visited forensic scientists and police departments in Rome, Berlin, New York, and Chicago.

Locard returned to Lyons both disappointed and determined. From what he could see, the science of crime detection was at a virtual standstill. At that time, there was still an ongoing debate about whether fingerprinting should replace bertillonage. Aside from that, no one in law enforcement anywhere seemed to be interested in putting Lacassagne's or Gross's or Doyle's ideas to use.

Locard refused to accept the situation. He vowed to change it. He decided to set an example by creating what he called a "police science," with its own principles and methods. He would include everything that science had to offer criminal investigation and bring this new police science to life.

Englishman Arthur Conan Doyle wrote the Sherlock Holmes detective stories.

Loccard began by describing his ideas in an article, which he showed to the Lyons police. They were not impressed. Bertillonage was good enough for them, they said. The attitude of the French police toward science had changed very little since the days of Eugene Francois Vidocq. Good police work was the result of cunning, knowledge of the streets, and tough interrogation, Locard was told. Science had its place in criminal investigation, but not a prominent place.

Locard would not give up, however. He kept pestering the Lyons police with his vision of a crime laboratory. He also kept working on new scientific techniques to help identify criminals.

One of these techniques was a refinement of Edward Henry's fingerprint system. Locard called it *poroscopy*. Pores are located along the tops of the skin ridges that make up the black lines of a fingerprint. Their purpose is to release perspiration to help cool the body. With the aid of a microscope, Locard isolated an area on the fingertip and counted the pores along a set of ridges. By performing this painstaking task, Locard discovered that 1 square inch (6.4 sq. cm) of ridge surface contains an average of 2,700 pores. More importantly, if the number of pores on the same section in two different fingerprints was identical, then the prints were a match.

Locard's poroscopy method was used in several criminal cases, but it was eventually abandoned. Edward Henry's system of classifying fingerprints was effective enough without it. But this and other research work got Locard noticed. With the help of this publicity, Locard's persistence eventually paid off.

In the summer of 1910, at the age of 33, Locard was given two paid assistants and two attic rooms on the fourth floor of the Palais de Justice, the Lyons Law Courts building. The rooms were dreary and dirty, and Locard had to buy his own equipment. It was far from the state-of-the-art crime laboratory he'd hoped for, but it was a start.

Now, like Bertillon and Henry before him, Locard needed a lucky break. That lucky break was the 1911 Counterfeiters Case. After solving that case, Locard was treated like a real-life Sherlock Holmes. In Doyle's stories, the London police took their most baffling cases to Sherlock Holmes. The supersleuth would then solve the crime using evidence the police had overlooked.

In 1912, the Lyons police came to Locard with a difficult murder case. Emile Gourbin, a bank clerk from Lyons, was suspected of killing his girlfriend. But Gourbin had an alibi. He insisted that he had been playing cards with friends at the time of the murder, and his friends backed up his story. The police thought Gourbin's friends were lying, but they couldn't prove it. Could Locard?

The victim had scratches on her neck, so Locard went to Gourbin's jail cell and scraped dirt from under the suspect's fingernails. When Locard analyzed the scrapings under a microscope, he found tiny flakes of skin. They might be skin from the victim's neck, but then again they might not be. The suspect could claim that the skin was his own—that he'd scratched himself. Was there anything about these skin scrapings that could tie them to the victim?

On closer examination, Locard noticed a faint sheen. It looked as if the flakes of skin had been colored in some way. Locard then noticed microscopic crystalline grains among the scrapings. Testing showed that the grains were composed of substances often used in cosmetics.

Locard had the police bring him every article of makeup from the dead girl's room. He was especially interested in a box of pink face powder. The girl used this powder daily, her mother said. A local pharmacist mixed it especially for her.

Locard went to see the pharmacist in his shop. What ingredients had he used to make the powder for the girl? The pharmacist made a list, and Locard looked it over. They were the same substances Locard had found in the scrapings taken from underneath the suspect's fingernails.

When Gourbin heard the evidence against him, he confessed. He'd strangled the girl in a jealous rage. Then he'd manufactured an alibi by turning the clock ahead in his friends' house. As a result, the friends thought Gourbin was with them at the time of the murder.

The Gourbin case brought Locard true and lasting respect. It also brought him additional funding and staff. Now Locard could leave most of the everyday work of the crime lab to his assistants.

This gave him time to devote to his great and lasting passion—dust. "When we reflect on the matter," Locard wrote, "we are startled that we should have been so tardy at carrying out so simple an idea: gathering the dust from an article of clothing and discovering from it which objects the suspected person brushed past and touched. For the microscopically finest particles that cover our clothing and our bodies are the mute witnesses to each of our movements and encounters."[3]

Locard devoted the next decade of his life to the study of dust. He made a vast collection of types of dust. It included samples from every known metal and every part of every known plant. At the same time, Locard continued improving methods for collecting and analyzing

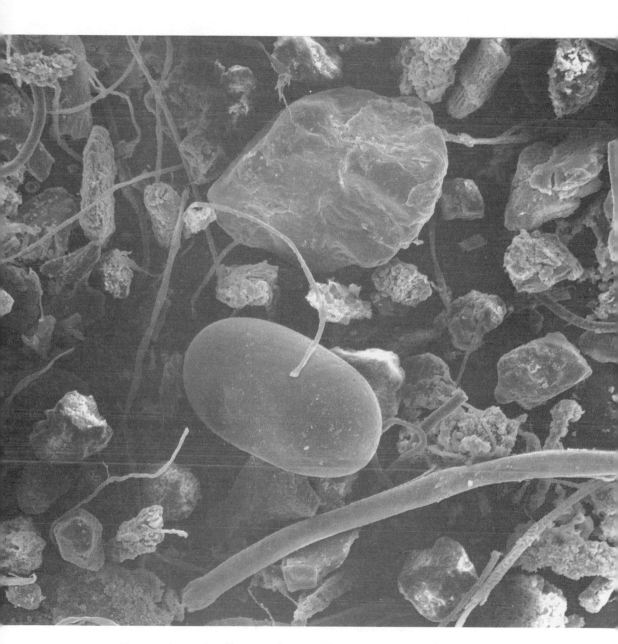

Human skin, nylon fibers, cat fur, sand, and flea droppings are revealed in this microscopic view of household dust collected from a vacuum cleaner.

this trace evidence. He developed detailed instructions for handling trace evidence.

- Never turn pants pockets inside out to see what's in them. Instead, carefully remove each pocket at the seams. Then pick off each particle of dust, one at a time, with tweezers.

- Collect these dust particles on pieces of paper. Then separate them into components, using magnets to pick out the particles of metal.

- Never scrape the dirt and dust from a suspect's shoes. Instead, remove it layer by layer.

- Keep each layer on a separate sheet of paper, numbered in its proper order.

In one case, Locard proved by examining the suspect's shoes that a murder suspect had walked to and from the scene of the crime— a flour mill. Locard found a layer of flour particles on the soles, sandwiched between layers of soil.

All this careful work resulted in what Locard called his exchange principle, which is still quoted in police work today: "Objects or surfaces which come into contact always exchange trace evidence. Every contact leaves a trace."[4]

Everyone who enters the scene of a crime takes something from the crime scene with them and leaves something of themselves behind. They might leave fingerprints or hairs. They might take with them a spot of the victim's blood on their clothing, or flakes of the victim's skin beneath their nails. They might take away fibers from the carpet on their shoes. They might leave behind footprints or tire tracks. These exchanges between criminals and victims are what detectives look for when they examine a crime scene.

Thanks to the work of Locard and his teachers—Lacassagne, Gross, and Doyle—modern forensic laboratories keep detailed files of tires and tire treads, vehicle paints and household paints, carpet fibers and fabric fibers, hair samples and handwriting samples, pollen samples and dust samples, and many other items.

Modern police files are far more numerous and detailed than the collection Locard accumulated in his little two-room crime laboratory in Lyons. But the purpose behind them is the same—to identify the people associated with them. "To write the history of identification," Locard wrote, "is to write the history of criminology."[5]

CHAPTER 5
"DEATH IS THE UGLIEST THING"

Clyde Snow and the Tales Skeletons Tell

The year was 1937. Nine-year-old Clyde Snow and his father, a Texas country doctor, were staying at a hunting lodge when two hunters discovered a human skeleton in the woods nearby.

Clyde, known then by the nickname Sonny, went along with his father and the local deputy sheriff for a look. He'd expected to see a bunch of white bones—like he'd seen in the movies and comic books, but what he saw surprised him. The bones were brown.

"Why?" he asked. His father explained that the bones hadn't been there long enough for the sun to bleach them.

As Sonny's father examined the bones for clues to the cause of death, the boy saw *forensic anthropology* in action for the first time. The human bones were mixed with the bones of a deer, so Dr. Snow concluded that the human skeleton was that of a hunter who suffered a fatal heart attack while trying to drag the large animal from the woods.

The deputy sheriff told Sonny and his father that a local man who liked to hunt had recently been reported missing. Dr. Snow found a set of keys among the bones, so the deputy drove to the man's house and tried to unlock the front door with the keys. One of the keys fit the lock perfectly. Dr. Snow had solved the mystery of the skeleton in the woods by "reading" the bones.

Since that memorable day, Clyde Snow has had personal encounters with thousands of human skeletons. His early experience influenced him so much that he decided to become a forensic anthropologist. He studies human skeletal remains as a way of discovering the identity of the victim and the cause of death.

A forensic anthropologist must be a highly disciplined individual whose mind is packed with all sorts of information. Sonny Snow was not a good student, however. His grades were poor, and he lacked self-discipline. In fact, he was actually expelled from high school for setting off firecrackers during an assembly. But Sonny had one quality that is essential for a successful career in forensic anthropology—an insatiable curiosity. Sonny had always been a curious child. For example, when his parents weren't looking, he would sneak his Christmas presents into his father's examining room to x-ray them.

After Sonny was expelled from high school, his parents sent him to a military school. This is when his attitude began to change. Clyde Snow, as he is known now, had a roommate who taught him how to study. This demanding roommate, an older boy, insisted that Clyde keep notes on index cards and stay up late at night memorizing the information. Clyde amazed himself as well as his parents by getting straight A's. Clyde continued to be a disciplined student all the way through college.

After graduation, Snow went to work for the Federal Aviation Administration (FAA). One of his duties was to search airplane crash sites for victims and piece the body parts together. This demanding task helped Clyde Snow develop another important quality—extreme and unrelenting patience.

In 1979, Snow's curiosity, independence, discipline, and patience were put to the test. On May 25, American Airlines Flight 191 left Chicago's O'Hare International Airport bound for Los Angeles. During takeoff, the engine and part of one wing broke away. Moments later, the rest of the McDonnell-Douglas DC-10 crashed.

All 258 passengers, 13 crew members, and 2 bystanders were killed instantly—273 victims in all. A Chicago fireman described the scene. "We didn't see one body intact . . . just trunks, hands, arms, heads, and parts of legs."[1] There were between 10,000 and 12,000 body parts to examine. It was clearly one of the worst air disasters in U.S. history.

Snow was part of the team of X-ray technicians, dentists, and medical investigators who pieced together and identified the bodies. Once the task was complete, the victims' families could lay their loved ones to rest. This is when Snow learned that a forensic anthropologist must have a strong stomach and be able to keep emotions under control in the face of unimaginable horror.

To aid them in their search, Snow's team had the victims' medical and dental records. But they had trouble finding the information that they needed quickly. For example, if they had a corpse that was 5 feet 9 inches (175 cm) tall, they had to check each victim's file for height. That process took a lot of time. They had to do the same thing for every piece of information for all 273 victims.

Clyde Snow had an idea—a way to make all these bits of information easier to access. A computer programmer from American Airlines listened to Snow's ideas, and went to work.

Firemen tag remains of corpses from Flight 191.

79

The result was a revolutionary computer program for keeping track of information about disaster victims. This information included physical descriptions from family and friends, each victim's height and weight, X rays, dental records, whether the person was right-handed or left-handed, and whether the person suffered any broken or fractured bones during his or her lifetime.

Using this program, Snow began examining the victims' remains, one set at a time. The bones in each set of remains were pieced together and measured with calipers and micrometers. These instruments were remarkably similar to the instruments that Bertillon had used in his pioneering forensic work 100 years earlier.

Snow then set about *parsing* the skeletons—drawing conclusions about the victims from their skeletal remains. In this process, the bones are examined with certain specific questions in mind.

Which sex was this person?

The size and shape of the bones provide clues. The bones of males tend to be broader at the ends than the bones of females. And the *supraorbital*, the bony ridge that makes up the brow, is generally larger and more prominent in males. On the other hand, the female pelvis tends to be broader than that of the male.

Which race was this person?

Just like the flesh-and-blood face it covers, the bony skull has features that point to one of the three major racial groupings—*Mongoloid, Negroid,* or *Caucasoid.* These features include the bony ridge at the bottom of the nose, which is generally higher in Caucasians than in other races, and the nasal margins, which are usually smoother in Mongoloids.

How old was this person?

If you look up inside a skull, you will notice a joint between the two major bones that form the top. In a child, this *basilar joint* is open to allow for growth. In an adult, the joint is closed. If you turn the skull over and look at the top, you will see zigzagging lines called *cranial sutures*. In general, the wider these sutures, the younger the person.

How tall was this person?

The fictional detective Sherlock Holmes could flawlessly deduce a person's height by measuring the length of his or her stride. Real-life bone detectives like Clyde Snow can deduce a person's height by measuring the long limb bone, the *femur*, and applying a mathematical formula to the result.

After Snow and his team had finished parsing the skeletons, they entered the information into the computer. The computer program then compared that information to the victims' medical records. For each skeleton, the computer printed out a list of ten victims whose descriptions came closest to matching that skeleton.

When the team finished its work, only 29 of the 273 victims of Flight 191 remained unidentified. Given the disastrous disorder that the team had to contend with, this was a truly remarkable achievement. Out of this terrible tragedy came Clyde Snow's pioneering computer program, which forensic scientists would use again and again in years to come when dealing with disaster victims.

At the same time that Snow was identifying the victims of one of the worst air tragedies in U.S. history, he was also identifying the victims of the worst mass murderer in U.S. history. On December 13, 1978, in Des Plaines, Illinois, police discovered the first of thirty-three bodies. All were young men in their teens and 20s. The killer, John Wayne Gacy, would not—or could not—identify the victims. Most were presumed to be runaways with few family ties.

Identifying these victims from their skeletal remains was a difficult task. After months of grueling work, Snow and his team had managed to identify twenty-four of Gacy's victims. "Death is the ugliest thing in the world," Snow said, thinking back on the experience.[2]

Gacy was not the only killer Snow has dealt with. His work in forensic anthropology has brought him face to face with a number of murderers. The most monstrous of them all was Josef Mengele. Mengele was more than a murderer. He was an exterminator of human beings. Mengele did his killing during the reign of Adolf Hitler, the dictator of Germany from 1933 to 1945. Hitler oversaw the *Holocaust*, the mass slaughter of 6 million European civilians, most of whom were Jews, by the Nazi party during World War II (1939–1945). Most of the victims were starved or gassed at death camps in Germany and Poland, and then cremated or buried in mass graves.

Known as Hitler's "Angel of Death," Mengele ran Auschwitz, the most notorious death camp and personally supervised the deaths of some 400,000 men, women, and children.

After Germany's defeat in 1945, Mengele fled to South America. For the next 30 years, people in ten dif-

To forensic anthropologist Clyde Snow, a skull holds vital clues to the former owner's identity.

83

ferent countries reported seeing Mengele, but the world's most-wanted murderer eluded capture.

In June 1985, Clyde Snow was asked by officials of the U.S. Justice Department to fly to Brazil. The Brazilian police had just opened a tomb. They claimed it held the skeletal remains of Hitler's Angel of Death.

When Snow arrived at the Medico-Legal Institute in São Paulo, he found that the police had made a mess of the remains. "What you need to use is the same sort of painstaking, methodical technique that archaeologists have used for 100 years in excavating prehistoric remains," Snow said.[3] Instead, the police had simply dug up the bones with picks and shovels. As a result, many of the bones had shattered.

Working with a team that included West German forensic anthropologist Richard Helmer, Snow had the bones reassembled and the skeleton parsed. The team then compared the results with the historical records on Mengele.

They had little to go on. Mengele's dental chart was no more than a crude drawing. It noted that there were twelve fillings, but said nothing about which teeth they were in. The medical records did not include an X ray.

Snow decided that they would have to use a forensic science technique known as *video skull-face superimposition*. The key would be Mengele's skull. It had been shattered by a gravedigger's shovel, but, using tweezers and glue, Helmer had painstakingly reassembled it. Snow had used springs and hinges to join the jaws.

In its own way, a skull is as unique as a fingerprint. The cheekbones may be high or low, flat or curving. The brow may be broad or narrow. The eyesockets of one skull may be closer together or farther apart than those of another skull. A face fits the skull from which it came— and no other.

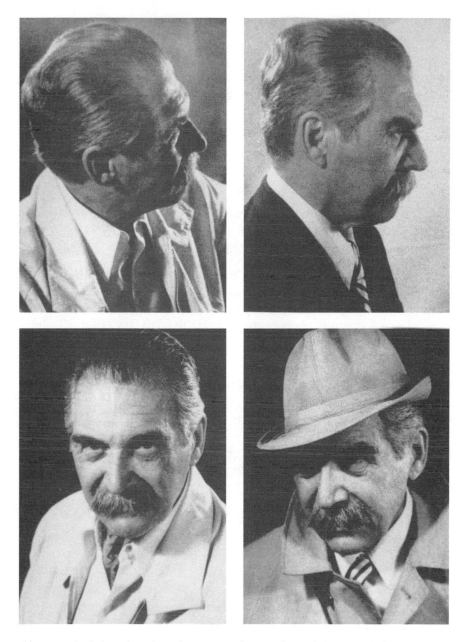

Photographs believed to show fugitive Josef Mengele, Hitler's "Angel of Death," near the end of his life

Helmer took the skull and an old photograph of Mengele and marked them both at the same thirty points. To mark the skull, he secured pins to the bone with dabs of clay. Helmer then mounted the marked skull on an aluminum post in a room in the Medico-Legal Institute. Next to it, on another post, he mounted Mengele's marked photograph.

Two high-resolution video cameras were set up on metal tracks at the back of the room. One camera was trained on the skull, the other on the photograph. The images from both cameras were fed through a video processor onto a single television screen. Helmer slid the cameras back and forth on their tracks until the two images, skull and photograph, were superimposed—one upon the other.

For a positive identification, all thirty points on both skull and photograph must line up precisely. Helmer peered at the ghostly results on the screen. The smiling face of Hitler's Angel of Death hovered over the smiling skull. All thirty points aligned exactly.

That evening, the team met to write their report. At Snow's suggestion, they reviewed and noted every last shred of evidence. Their conclusion was unanimous. This was indeed Josef Mengele.

A year later, Mengele's dental X rays were discovered and compared with the skull's teeth. Everything matched. The findings of Snow and his team were confirmed.

Like other forensic anthropologists, Snow used science to identify victims of disasters and violent crimes and, in the case of Mengele, the perpetrator of horrendous crimes. But Snow also put his skills and the tools of his trade to unusual uses. In one case, his findings revised a piece of American history.

In Montana, just west of the Black Hills of South Dakota, lies the Custer Battlefield, where the Battle of the Little Bighorn was fought on June 25, 1876. On that day, General George Armstrong Custer and all 267 of his soldiers and scouts were killed. It was a battle the Sioux and Cheyenne Indians won in a war they were destined to lose.

More than 100 years later, this event still intrigued people. Since Custer and all his men had died, there was no one to give their side of the story. That would have to

At the Battle of the Little Bighorn, General George Armstrong Custer and his 267 soldiers and scouts were killed.

be pieced together from whatever evidence could be found at the site.

In 1983, a brushfire burned off the battlefield's outer skin of prairie grass and uncovered new artifacts. Among them were bones of Custer's soldiers. Clyde Snow was asked by archaeologists from the National Park Service to examine these bones. He jumped at the opportunity. Snow was always looking for new and different ways to put the science of forensic anthropology to work.

The bones had been discovered at a spot where a troop of twenty to thirty of Custer's men were believed to have been killed, then buried. Most of the bones were widely scattered, but one skeleton was recovered nearly intact. Snow's team named this skeleton "Mike."

In the 100-plus years since the battle, all the known historical records of Custer's men had been gathered. When "Mike's" bones were reassembled, they told a great deal about their former owner. In fact, only one man from these historical records fit Mike's description.

"Mike" turned out to be Mitch Boyer, one of Custer's scouts. Snow drew this conclusion after carefully parsing the skeleton. One telling clue came from the skull's teeth. The arched marks on the left incisor and canine teeth were characteristic of a habitual pipe smoker, something Boyer was known for. The marks came from his habit of clenching the pipe stem between his teeth.

Indians who had fought in the battle had said that Boyer's detachment of troops had been killed at another location, a good distance from where Boyer's bones were found. Snow's identification of Boyer meant that a part of American history had to be rewritten.

Snow's curiosity was struck by the skeletal remains of another of Custer's soldiers. He saw the skull, left arm, rib, and two vertebrae on display in a museum near the battlesite. Snow had a cast made of the skull and took it back with him to Oklahoma, where he lived. There he met with Betty Pat Gatliff, an old friend and colleague, to put a face on the soldier's skull.

Gatliff was a medical artist and sculptor. Her office was unofficially known as the SKULLpture lab. Snow and Gatliff had been working together for more than two decades. During that time, Gatliff had become a pioneer in the art of *facial reconstruction*.

Forensic scientists from the late 1800s, such as Bertillon and Galton and Lacassagne, were fascinated by the landscape of the human body. And some of them performed what now seem like gruesome experiments on human bodies.

One German scientist, a man named His, plunged a series of oiled needles into the faces of corpses. At the top of each needle, His had fastened a cork. When the needle hit bone, he would slide the cork down to the skin surface. Then he pulled the needle out, measured the length of the needle below the cork, and noted the position and depth on a drawing of the face. The result was a kind of depth map of the face.

This process could be compared to dropping a weighted line at different spots in a lake in order to plot the lake's depth at different points. From these experiments, His learned two important facts. The depth of skin on a person's face varies from one point to another, but these variations are nearly identical in all human faces. Although forensic anthropologists still do research in this area, known as tissue-depth measurement, they now use painless ultrasound techniques on living subjects.

Using tissue-depth information, a skilled facial reconstructionist like Betty Pat Gatliff can design a skinlike covering for a skull. This is exactly what she did for the skull cast that Snow brought back from the Custer Battlefield. First, she broke eraser heads off pencils and cut them to different lengths. She glued these eraser heads to the soldier's skull in eighteen places and connected them with strips of clay in a grid. She then filled the spaces in this grid with clay to form the face's distinctive features. Gatliff always puts a smile on the faces because, she says, a smile reveals the teeth and helps bring a face to life. The false teeth and eyes came from medical-supply companies. The hair was an appropriately colored wig.

The face Gatliff produced from the cast of the soldier's skull was handsome—broad-nosed, wide-mouthed, and strong-jawed. Over the years, historians had managed to collect pictures of most of Custer's men. The sculpted face was a remarkable match for the face of Miles O'Hara. The details Snow had gathered from parsing the soldier's remains matched what was known of O'Hara, including his height and age. "Bones make good witnesses," Snow said. "Although they speak softly, they never lie and they never forget."[4]

Snow put forensic anthropology to another unusual use when he was asked to aid in the fight against human rights abuses by repressive governments. From 1976 to 1983, Argentina was ruled by a military government that had, in effect, declared war on its own people.

During those years, more than 10,000 Argentineans vanished. They came to be known as the *desaparecidos*, which means "the disappeared." Military police arrived at their homes in unmarked cars and took these people to one of 360 detention centers. There, they were tortured and sometimes killed. Their bodies were buried in graves marked N.N. for "no nombre," which means "no name."

What had these desaparecidos done to deserve torture and even death? Some had been openly critical of their country's government. Others were suspected of

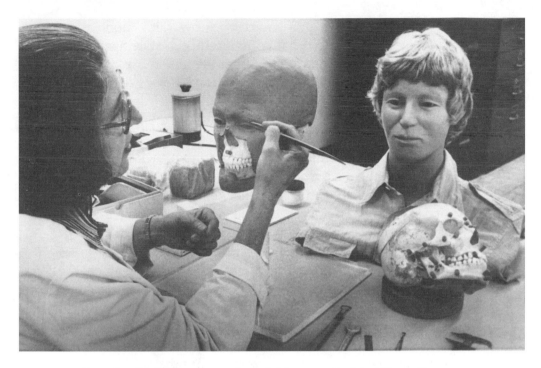

Betty Pat Gatliff reconstructs the facial features of a John Wayne Gacy murder victim.

being critical. Still others were just ordinary citizens. No one was safe.

"First, we will kill all the subversives," one military official said, "then we will kill their collaborators, then their sympathizers, then those who remain indifferent, and finally, we will kill the timid."[5]

All this changed in 1984 when a civilian government came to power. Suddenly, ordinary citizens could begin to feel safe in their homes. But what about all the damage that had been done and the men who had done it? In May of that year, Clyde Snow was contacted by an international human rights group. What they told him about the desaparecidos hit a nerve.

"Of all the forms of murder," Snow said, "none is more monstrous than that committed by a state against its own citizens. And of all murder victims, those of the state are the most helpless and vulnerable, since the very entity to which they have entrusted their lives and safety becomes their killer."[6]

In June 1984, Clyde Snow arrived in Argentina. He came to identify the desaparecidos so that their families could give them a proper burial. But that wasn't the only reason Snow had come. First, the victims must be identified. Later on, Snow vowed, the people responsible for their deaths would be put on trial, and the bones of their victims would convict them. Snow would use forensic science in a new and startling way. He would put an entire government on trial.

No Argentinean professionals dared to work with Snow, but he did manage to find five young Argentine medical students to assist him. "They knew they'd be sticking their necks out," Snow said. "But they did it."[7]

Because Argentina is in the Southern Hemisphere, June falls in the middle of the winter. When Snow and the students arrived at Boulogne Cemetery in the Buenos Aires suburb of San Isidro, it was a cold, crisp, sunny morning. The team quickly located what they were looking for—a grave marked N.N. Desaparecidos were said to be buried there. This was a combination crime scene and archaeological site, Snow told his assistants. It must be treated with care and investigated methodically.

First, Snow and his shivering young assistants divided the gravesite into grids. Then they began sifting through the soil in each sector. After digging down 4 inches (10 cm), the team laid planks across the hole. Then, lying over the planks, they reached down and gently began to scrape the soil away with trowels and spoons.

One hour later, they hit the first bone. After a moment, however, they realized it belonged to a cow. Then they found a coffin. Inside the coffin, they found a skull, and in the skull, they found a bullet hole. "Right above the eye," Snow remembers. "There was an earthworm right next to it."[8]

It took the rest of the day to uncover the entire skeleton. First, Snow photographed the remains where they lay. Then each bone was carefully removed, cataloged, and packed in a plastic bag.

Back in the morgue in Buenos Aires, everything was laid out on an autopsy table, where Snow parsed the skeleton. It belonged to a woman, he concluded. He also noted her age and height and confirmed that the hole in the skull had come from a bullet.

Snow was never able to identify this particular victim's remains. But a year later, at another cemetery, he uncovered the remains of Liliana Carmen Pereyra, a 21-year-old law student who had vanished in 1977. Snow identified her from dental and medical records.

Snow was also able to establish the cause of death. Officials of Argentina's former military government claimed that no one had been tortured at their hands, and that the missing people had simply fled to other countries, where they were hiding out. They also insisted that the victims found buried in unmarked graves had died in shootouts with security forces. Snow believed otherwise. Pereyra's skull had been shattered by a shotgun blast at close range—execution style.

"These people were murdered," Snow insisted. "Their bones are their only witnesses. And only we can help them to be heard."[9]

Snow also managed to identify other victims whose remains he unearthed from other cemeteries in Argentina. Snow believes that the living have a duty to

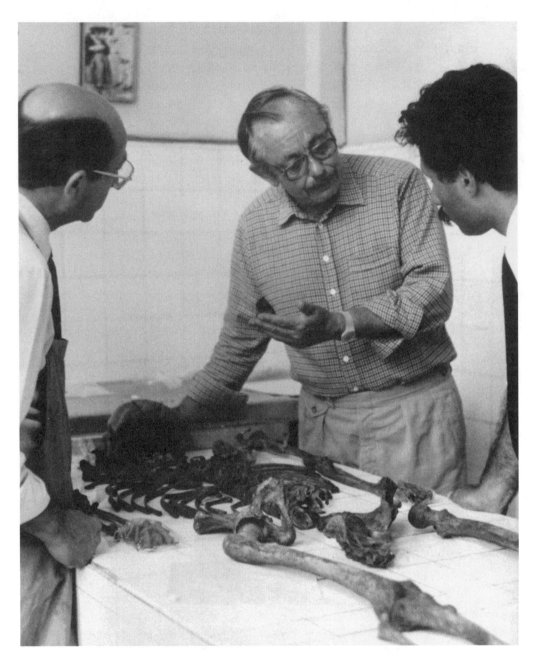

Forensic anthropologist Clyde Snow parses a skeleton.

learn from the dead, and to testify to what they have learned. When former government officials were put on trial, Snow was there to testify against them.

Seven high-ranking officials were convicted, with Clyde Snow serving as chief witness for the prosecution. One of the many telling details to which he testified were the bullet holes in the arms of the victims. When a gun is pointed at you, your natural reaction is to raise your arms. It was down-to-earth details like these that brought the reality of the situation home to judges and juries, and helped focus attention on the horrors of government by terror.

"The homicidal state shares one trait with the solitary killer," Snow said. "Like all murderers, it trips on its own egotism and drops a trail of clues which, when properly collected, preserved, and analyzed, are as damning as a signed confession left in the grave."[10]

Clyde Snow is a different sort of forensic science pioneer. Alphonse Bertillon, Edward Henry, Karl Landsteiner, and Edmond Locard all developed new technologies. They pioneered new methods and techniques for identifying people. Snow's pioneering efforts have less to do with technology and more to do with passion. Snow's work on the Custer Battlefield and in the cemeteries of Argentina is the work of a man with a mission. Snow uses forensic science to understand the past and to help shape the future.

Not everyone who uses science in new ways sets out to become a pioneer, though. Another forensic scientist, a young British *geneticist*, set out to accomplish one small goal and ended up developing a whole new area of forensic science.

CHAPTER 6

"OH GOD, WHAT HAVE WE DONE HERE?"

Alec Jeffreys and the Great DNA Manhunt

Ayoung scientist named Alec Jeffreys stood anxiously waiting in his laboratory. It was Monday, September 15, 1984, in Leicester, England. Jeffreys was waiting for a batch of X-ray film to finish developing. He had tackled a difficult research problem from a new angle and was hoping the solution would show up on the X-ray film.

Like other scientists before him, Jeffreys was investigating human identity. What was it that made each of us unmistakably unique? Alphonse Bertillon had worked with the outer body; Edward Henry had used the patterns on the tips of the fingers; Karl Landsteiner had worked with blood; and Clyde Snow had examined skeletons.

But Alec Jeffreys was working with something that permeates every last bit of us. He was working with a substance so tiny that it must be magnified millions of times to be seen. Jeffreys was working with *deoxyribonucleic acid* (DNA). DNA is everywhere in us, and it

Alec Jeffreys in his laboratory

comes out in everything that comes out of us. We are constantly oozing and losing DNA. It's in the skin cells we shed and the hairs that come off on our combs. It's in the *saliva* we leave on the rims of the glasses we drink from and on the flaps of the envelopes we lick. It's in our blood and our sweat and our urine. It's also in semen and *vaginal fluid*. It's even in our tears. Nearly every one of the 10 trillion cells in our bodies contains DNA.

Why was Jeffreys so interested in DNA? What part does DNA play in establishing human identity? The answers lie deep within our cells. Inside each cell is a watery *nucleus* containing twenty-three pairs of *chromosomes*. A chromosome contains long strands of tightly coiled DNA. DNA is made of small units called *nucleotides*. Each nucleotide contains a sugar, a phosphate, and a base. These units join together to create a DNA molecule shaped like a spiraling ladder. Scientists call this shape a *double helix*.

There are four different kinds of bases in DNA: guanine (G), cytosine (C), thymine (T), and adenine (A). These nucleotide bases, which join together to form the rungs of the DNA ladder, carry instructions for making *amino acids*. A segment of DNA that carries all the information needed to string a group of amino acids into a protein is called a *gene*.

Because proteins are the chief building blocks of our cells, the set of instructions contained in our genes determine who we are and what we look like. As you can see, DNA is a very important molecule. As one science writer puts it, "Blue eyes, brown hair, short, tall, thin, fat are all said to be encoded in this fabulously complex molecule."[1]

During reproduction, chromosomes carry all the information contained in our genes from parent to child. When scientists want to talk about all the genes on all

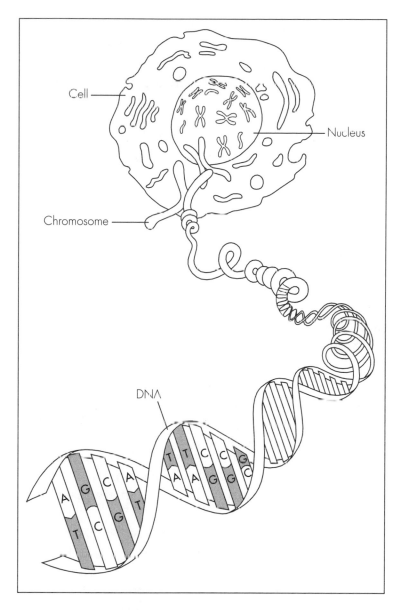

The nucleus of every human cell contains twenty-three pairs of chromosomes. A chromosome contains long chains of DNA nucleotides. There are four different kinds of nucleotide bases: guanine (G), cytosine (C), thymine (T), and adenine (A).

our chromosomes, they use the word *genome*. The human genome contains about 100,000 genes and about 3 billion nucleotides.

Scientists sometimes compare a person's genome to computer software. Your genome contains a "program" that tells your body what to do and how to do it. Without this program, you would not be able to tie your shoes, eat your lunch, or grow into an adult. A person's genome can also be compared to the letters that form the words in a book of instructions. The letters that make up our DNA book of instructions are the bases—G, C, T, and A.

Nearly all the instructions in your genome are identical to the instructions in every other person's genome— only about 0.01 percent are different. You shouldn't be too surprised by that. After all, we are all members of the same species. We all look very similar and function in pretty much the same way. We all have one head with two eyes, a nose, a mouth, and two ears. This head is connected to a body with two arms and two legs. Each hand has ten fingers, and each foot has ten toes. We all have lungs that breathe, hearts that beat, and blood that flows.

There are a lot of things we have in common, but there are also many differences between people. Geneticist Eric Lander explained it this way during a lecture.

> Look at the neighbor to your left and to your right. You're 99.9 percent identical. But in a genome of 3 billion letters, even 0.01 percent difference translates into 3 million separate spelling differences. I invite you again to look to the left and look to the right and notice how unique you are. There is no one in this audience who has the same DNA sequence as anyone else.[2]

This is what Alec Jeffreys was investigating that September morning in 1984 in his laboratory. He was trying to catch a glimpse of the 3 million unique rungs on the DNA ladder. He wanted to see exactly what makes each person different from everyone else.

According to Jeffreys, it was a quest that began when he was just a child. "My interest in genetics and *biochemistry* began at the age of seven, when my father presented me with a microscope and a remarkably lethal chemistry set," he said. "I followed this growing interest in chemistry and biology throughout my schooldays and became particularly interested in the interface between the two subjects."[3]

Now, 27 years later, Jeffreys was close to success. He knew that a person's 3 million unique rungs are not found all together in one place. They are scattered here and there throughout the 3 billion rungs that make up a person's entire genome. They are located in what scientists call *hypervariable regions*. These hypervariable regions of DNA are a tantalizing puzzle to geneticists like Jeffreys. These regions do not contain genes that issue instructions for assembling proteins. They are not part of the body's internal "software."

What do they do then? Why are they there? Scientists cannot answer these questions. Hypervariable regions have no known function, which is why some scientists call them "junk DNA." When Jeffreys learned about hypervariable regions, he realized that it might not be junk at all. In fact, it might be very useful. Since hypervariable regions are unique in each person, he thought it might be possible to use them to establish identity.

Jeffreys didn't expect to learn a great deal about these hypervariable regions in one morning. Other geneticists had tried mapping them, with little success. All he could realistically hope for was a few glimpses on the X-ray film—the beginnings of a map of these mysterious, uncharted regions of the genome.

Jeffreys' hopes rested on specially designed genetic markers. These markers consisted of sequences of hypervariable DNA that Jeffreys had managed to collect. They were supposed to operate like homing devices, traveling along the genome's twisted ladder until they located hypervariable regions like themselves. They were then supposed to attach themselves to these regions. Since Jeffreys had made the markers radioactive, they—and the hypervariable regions of DNA they found—should be visible on the X-ray film.

When the film was ready, Jeffreys pulled it from the developing tank and lay it out for viewing. His research assistants gathered around to look at it with him. Jeffreys' markers had done far, far better than anyone expected.

"Oh God," Jeffreys said, "What have we done here?"[4]

Instead of a few isolated images on the film, they saw a whole complex of patterns. They stared at the series of gray and black bands stacked on top of one another. Like the bar codes they put on products in supermarkets, Jeffreys thought.

What did these mysterious markings mean?

Years later, thinking back on that day, Jeffreys recalls that "We'd been looking for good genetic markers for basic genetic analysis and had stumbled on a way of establishing a human's genetic identification. By the afternoon we'd named our discovery *DNA fingerprinting*."[5]

Like the prints on the tips of the fingers, these hypervariable regions of DNA were unique. Your DNA fingerprint, Jeffreys said, "does not belong to anyone else on the face of this planet who ever has been or ever will be."[6]

Hoping for nothing more than a glimpse, Jeffreys had stumbled onto the entire picture. "It was a classic case of basic science coming up with a technology which could be applied to a problem in an unanticipated way," he said.[7]

By "technology," Jeffreys meant his process of using radioactive markers to locate hypervariable regions of DNA. He called this process *RFLP* (restriction fragment length polymorphism), or "Riflips."

In addition to being a research scientist, Jeffreys was an entrepreneur. Realizing he was onto something that could make him a wealthy man, he applied for a patent on his RFLP process. But what exactly could this process be used for? Jeffreys wasn't sure yet. He would have to test and refine the process first.

Jeffreys did this by conducting numerous experiments. In the process, he discovered that a person's DNA fingerprint was the same no matter what kind of cells were tested. Blood cells, skin cells, saliva cells, semen cells, and bone cells all produced the same result. And Jeffreys found that he could obtain a DNA fingerprint from the tiniest traces of tissue, even a speck of 3-year-old dried blood.

Imagine what DNA fingerprinting could do for forensic science! According to Edmond Locard's exchange principle, anyone at the scene of a crime takes something away and leaves something behind. Now forensic scientists could determine a criminal's identity from flakes of skin under the victim's fingernails, a piece of hair, or even a drop of blood. The tiniest bit of tissue would be enough to obtain a DNA fingerprint and a positive identification.

But Jeffreys had no great interest in murder cases or crime. He made no special effort to get the police interested in his process. But 2 years later—in 1986—the police came to him. By that time, Jeffreys and his research team had refined the RFLP process. "These patterns are now much simpler to read and interpret," Jeffreys said, "and you can store them on a computer database. You can also develop them using much less DNA."[8] The time was right for Jeffreys' system to be tested in a criminal case.

Two 15-year-old schoolgirls, Lynda Mann and Dawn Ashworth, had been brutally raped and strangled less than 10 miles (16 km) from Jeffreys' laboratory. Although the murders had occurred 3 years apart, the police believed that the same person had committed both crimes. Unfortunately, they had no proof. No one had seen the girls murdered, and no fingerprints had been left at the crime scenes. The only physical evidence the police had was the killer's semen, which had been left on both girls' clothing.

The investigation focused on George Howard, an immature young man with a past record of minor sex offenses. He'd been seen near the crime scene the night Dawn Ashworth was killed. The police picked up Howard and took him to the station for questioning. The questioning continued through the morning and into the afternoon. At first, Howard admitted to seeing Dawn Ashworth, but not to killing her.

When the police suggested that Howard might have killed her unintentionally—that the killing had been an accident—Howard confessed. Yes, he said, he must have gone temporarily insane and killed her. However, Howard insisted he'd had nothing to do with Lynda Mann's death.

The Leicestershire police were stumped. They had no confession to the Mann murder and no convincing evidence for either crime. That's when they decided to ask Jeffreys for help. They had heard about Jeffreys' method of identifying a person from the tiniest bit of DNA material.

A detective inspector from the Leicestershire Constabulary sent samples of blood from George Howard and semen stains from the murdered girls' clothing to Jeffreys at his Leicester laboratory. Jeffreys tested the material. His RFLP method produced three clear DNA fingerprints: one from the semen stains on Ashworth's clothing, a second from the semen stains on Mann's clothing, and a third from George Howard's blood sample.

Jeffreys called the police into his Leicester laboratory and showed them the X-ray film of the three DNA fingerprints. Two were identical, but the third was entirely different. This third DNA fingerprint was the one obtained from George Howard's blood.

What did this mean? Jeffreys told the police the bad news. "Not only is your man innocent in the Mann case, he isn't even the man who killed Dawn Ashworth." Then he gave them the good news: "You only have to catch one killer. The same man murdered both girls." Jeffreys pointed to the DNA fingerprints from the semen stains. Each stripe of gray and black matched exactly. "We have here the signature of the real murderer."[9]

That murderer was not George Howard. A weak-willed suspect like Howard could be intimidated into making a false confession, but his DNA could not be intimidated into implicating him. George Howard had made a false confession. The real killer of Dawn Ashworth and Lynda Mann was still at large.

On November 21, 1986, George Howard was released from custody. On that day he took his place in the history of forensic science as the first man to be found innocent as a result of DNA fingerprinting. "If we hadn't developed the technology," said Alec Jeffreys, "I'm confident he would have been jailed for life."[10]

Meanwhile, the police were no closer to solving the case. Who was the real killer?

A scientist examines a DNA fingerprint.

They had his "signature," as Jeffreys put it, right there in front of them. But whose fingerprint was it? There were no files they could go to and pull up a matching DNA fingerprint with the owner's name on it. DNA fingerprints had never been used by the police. No records of DNA fingerprints existed anywhere.

The Leicestershire police would have to create those records. They would have to somehow obtain the killer's DNA fingerprint and match it to the one that Jeffreys had found on the murdered girls' clothing. But how? There were literally thousands of young men in the area. Any one of them could have killed the girls.

"We're going to try something that's never been done," said Chief Superintendent David Baker.[11] The Leicestershire police, along with Alec Jeffreys, were about to launch the world's first DNA-based manhunt. They intended to test the blood of men in the villages of

Narborough and Enderby, where the girls were found. They would also test men in the neighboring village of Littlethorpe. All male residents between the ages of 17 and 34 would be asked to submit a sample.

Legally, the police couldn't force anyone to cooperate. The tests would have to be voluntary. But there would be great social pressure to cooperate. The killer might strike again. The women in the area needed to be protected from the threat of rape and violent death. How could anyone but the killer himself refuse?

Unfortunately, that was the problem with the plan. It was highly unlikely that the killer would volunteer his blood. As one police official put it, "We just hoped that it might somehow flush him out."[12] They had to hope the killer would make some sort of slip.

Testing began in January 1987. The police were fanatically thorough. With thousands of samples to obtain, they had to be meticulous. Reporting stations were set up at hospitals and at doctor's offices, and a crew of mobile medical technicians drove to remote areas to collect samples. Some drove as many as 500 miles (800 km) a day.

Strange things happened along the way. A number of men with needle phobias had to be persuaded to cooperate. One man insisted that he'd rather be punched in the nose than pricked with a needle. Another fainted as he watched the blood being sucked out of his arm.

Eight months after the manhunt began, a total of 4,528 men had been tested. There were no matches. The police still had no suspect.

Then, on a summer evening in 1987, they got a lucky break. Men and women who worked in a local bakery were having drinks and talking at a pub. One of the men mentioned that a co-worker named Colin Pitchfork had persuaded him to take the blood test in his place, claiming to be Pitchfork.

When word of the switch reached the police on September 19, they questioned Pitchfork. Samples of the suspect's blood were sent to Jeffreys for testing. Pitchfork's DNA fingerprint proved to be a perfect match for the one obtained from the semen found on both victims' clothing. Colin Pitchfork became the first person to be

The first murderer uncovered and convicted by DNA fingerprinting evidence was Colin Pitchfork.

convicted of murder on the basis of DNA evidence. He was sentenced to two life terms. In passing sentence, the judge said that if it weren't for DNA, Pitchfork might never have been caught.

Alec Jeffreys could not have hoped for a more conclusive demonstration of the power of his discovery. An innocent man had been cleared. A guilty man had been caught and convicted. All of this had happened because of evidence provided by Jeffreys' RFLP process.

Newspapers all over the world picked up the story. DNA fingerprinting was now being widely used by law-enforcement agencies. It had become a formidable new tool of forensic science. Jeffreys' discovery was widely hailed as the most significant breakthrough in forensic science since the discovery of fingerprints.

A scientific discovery as potentially powerful as DNA fingerprinting is usually greeted with a great deal of enthusiasm and praise at first. After a while, though, people begin having doubts and asking questions. At first, Jeffreys' process was hailed as foolproof, though not by Jeffreys himself. He knew that no system operated by human beings can ever be foolproof. It wasn't long before human error started showing up in highly publicized court cases involving DNA fingerprinting and doubts about DNA evidence surfaced.

One such case, known as the Castro case, occurred in New York City in 1989. A woman and her daughter were stabbed to death in their apartment. A speck of blood had been found on the watch of the prime suspect, a neighbor named Castro. The blood on Castro's watch and the blood of the victims were tested by Lifecodes Lab. The DNA fingerprint from the blood on Castro's watch matched the DNA fingerprint of one of the victims.

The prosecution presented the Lifecodes lab results as prime evidence against the suspect. But the results were called into question by the defense. The lab had made a technical error in processing the evidence. As a result, the DNA results were declared invalid, and the prosecution's case fell apart. The suspect later confessed to the murders, removing any doubts that Lifecodes' results had been inaccurate. But the suspect's confession was not enough to keep doubts from surfacing.

These doubts about DNA evidence did not arise without reason. Because DNA technology had been introduced into the legal system in an excited rush, the scientific community had not had time to properly examine, test, judge, and regulate the complex technical procedures involved in Alec Jeffreys' RFLP process.

The public hadn't had time to get a grasp of the process either. As one public defender put it, "With a standard fingerprint you can put it up on the wall, you can blow it up, follow the ridges—great, it matches. An average juror looking at a DNA fingerprint doesn't even know what it is."[13]

The press picked up on these doubts. On January 29, 1990, the *New York Times* ran a front-page article headlined "Some Scientists Doubt the Value of 'Genetic Fingerprint' Evidence." According to the article, seven leading *molecular biologists* had stated that DNA analysis was too unreliable to be used in court. If the article had appeared in any other newspaper, it would not have caused much of a stir. But the *New York Times* has long been the newspaper of record in the United States—the most respected, most relied-upon source of information about national and international current events.

The article could have put an end to the use of DNA fingerprinting in court cases. Fortunately, four of the molecular biologists quoted in the article issued an immediate correction in a strongly worded letter to the *Times*. There is "excellent agreement among scientists that the validity of the DNA identification method is widely accepted," they wrote.[14]

Nevertheless, the controversy continued. The report on DNA testing that everyone had been waiting for was due to be issued in April 1992. The National Research Council Committee of the prestigious National Academy of Sciences had spent 2 years compiling it.

Two days before the report's official release date, the *New York Times* ran a front page story about it. The headline read "U.S. Panel Seeking Restriction on Use of DNA in Courts." Newspapers often run stories about important reports before they're officially released. They want to be the first newspaper with the story. But sometimes, in their haste to be first, they get the story wrong. The *Times* article said the committee's report would recommend that courts stop using DNA evidence until the DNA fingerprinting process could be looked at in more detail.

As with the 1990 story, reaction was swift. That same day, the chairman of the National Research Council Committee insisted that they had said nothing of the kind. Instead, the committee had concluded that DNA evidence should continue to be used without interruption. But they did believe that DNA testing should be "regulated and controlled by scientists and federal agencies that have no stake in the method's success or failure."[15]

The scientific community agreed. Strict standards were vital. Geneticist Eric Lander put it this way: "If I sneeze on something, my DNA is there, too. And so there is tremendous need to avoid contamination."[16]

Lander's words proved to be prophetic. Three years later, the standards DNA laboratories used in analyzing tissue samples were put to the test in "the trial of the century." Former football star O. J. Simpson stood accused of stabbing his former wife, Nicole Brown, and her friend, Ronald Goldman.

The prosecution's entire case was built on circumstantial evidence. The murder weapon was never recovered, no one had witnessed the murder, and Simpson insisted that he was innocent. But still, the evidence against Simpson looked overwhelming before the trial began. DNA testing showed conclusively that the bloodstains police had found on Simpson's car and at his home had come from the victims. The DNA fingerprints matched. The prosecution's case rested largely on this DNA-based evidence.

The Simpson evidence was analyzed using a technique known as *PCR* (polymerase chain reaction). PCR represented a significant improvement on Jeffreys' original RFLP method. Using PCR, testers could obtain a DNA fingerprint from a much smaller tissue sample in a matter of days rather than weeks. The secret was *cloning*. A tiny sample of cells could be cloned billions of times in a few hours, giving testers an abundance of DNA material to work with.

Simpson's defense team never disputed the PCR-DNA test results. Instead, they claimed that police had deliberately planted the victims' bloodstains on Simpson's car, at his home, and in the police laboratory where the DNA evidence was tested. They claimed it was all part of a conspiracy on the part of the Los Angeles police to frame Simpson.

The defense submitted no real evidence to prove that the police had in fact planted or contaminated any evi-

DNA evidence that might have convicted O. J. Simpson of murder was discounted by the jury.

dence. Their claims amounted to pure speculation. But the defense didn't have to offer any real evidence. All they had to do was offer the jury an alternate explanation for each piece of evidence against their client. If the jury found these explanations at all believable, they would have to acquit Simpson.

And that is what happened. On October 3, 1995, O. J. Simpson was acquitted because his defense team had managed to cast doubt on the motives of the police. But they had cast no doubt on the DNA evidence. No one argued that the DNA fingerprints from the case were anything but accurate and genuine.

Still, after the verdict in this highly publicized trail, it was inevitable that DNA evidence would continue to be challenged. After all, human errors are inevitable. But DNA evidence, properly obtained, has continued to be all but unchallengeable in the courts when it comes to the issue of establishing identity.

Since the Simpson verdict, governments of all fifty states in the United States have passed laws requiring sex offenders and other convicted criminals to provide blood samples so that their DNA fingerprints can be kept on file. By 1998, approximately 600,000 DNA fingerprints had been gathered from around the nation.

In that same year, the FBI launched a national computer system that eventually would link the databases of all fifty states. Now, DNA fingerprint evidence gathered at the scene of a violent crime can be compared to the DNA fingerprints on record in the database, and repeat offenders can be immediately identified.

In the years since Alec Jeffreys' historic discovery, DNA fingerprinting has been through a great many trials and refinements. The most notable of these refinements is the PCR process. Jeffreys is pleased with the result.

"The advantage of PCR," he says, "is that it offers great sensitivity, potential for automation, lower costs, and information that is much less ambiguous in terms of a *DNA profiling* result."[17]

Jeffreys knows that there will be other improvements on his discovery in years to come. Advancements in the technology of DNA fingerprinting will make the process even more efficient and accurate. After all, that is the nature of forensic science.

GLOSSARY

agglutination—see *clot*

amino acid—a building block of proteins

anarchy—a political and social movement calling for the end of all forms of government and law

anthropometry (bertillonage)—a systematic procedure of taking a series of body measurements as a means of distinguishing one individual from another

antibody—a protein substance that destroys or weakens bacteria

basilar joint—the joint between the two major bones that form the top of the skull

bertillonage—see *anthropometry*

biochemistry—the science dealing with the chemical processes of living matter

blood transfusion—the process of transferring blood from one person or other type of animal to another

blood typing—classifying a person's blood according to its blood type

calipers—an instrument used to measure thickness or diameter

Caucasoid—descendant of the original inhabitants of Europe, southwestern Asia, and northern Africa

cell—the basic unit of living matter from which all plants and animals are made

centrifuge—a machine with a wheel of test tubes connected to a central axis that spins at high speeds

chromosome—a body in the nucleus of a cell that carries hereditary information from parent to child

cloning—the asexual reproduction of cells genetically identical to one another

clot—to form clumps

counterfeit—a false copy of something, such as money, made in order to deceive

cranial suture—one of the zigzagging lines on the top of the skull where two bones join *criminology*—the scientific study of crime

deoxyribonucleic acid (DNA)—a double-stranded, spiraling molecule containing instructions for growth, development, and replication

desaparecidos—"the disappeared"; citizens tortured and killed by Argentina's military government between 1976 and 1983

DNA fingerprinting—the use of fragments of DNA to identify the unique genetic makeup of an individual

DNA profiling—see *DNA fingerprinting*

double helix—a common name for DNA, referring to the double-stranded, spiraling structure of the molecule

facial reconstruction—the forensic technique of simulating a victim's face by fitting a clay based mask onto the skull

femur—the long bone between the hip and the knee

fingerprinting—the forensic technique of using ink and paper to take the impressions of the markings on the inner surface of the last joint of a finger or thumb

forensic anthropology—the study of human skeletal remains as a way of discovering the identity of the victim and the cause of death

gene—the unit of heredity in chromosomes; a segment of DNA

geneticist—a scientist who studies genes

genome—all the genes that we possess

guillotine—a machine for beheading people by means of a heavy blade that slides down between a pair of posts

Holocaust—the extermination of 6 million European Jews during World War II

hypervariable regions—the areas of the human genome that vary most from person to person, also called "junk DNA"

hypothesis—a statement, usually an attempt to solve a problem, that seems true but must be tested in order to be proven true

latent—nearly invisible, hidden

microorganism—a microscopic organism, such as bacteria

minutiae—the small details of fingerprint patterns, such as forks, islands, and bridges

molecular biologist—a scientist who studies the structures of living organisms in terms of the composition and interaction of their molecules

molecule—the smallest particle into which an element can be divided without changing its properties

Mongoloid—descendant of the original inhabitants of the continent of Asia *naturalist*—person who makes a study of living organisms in their environment

Negroid—descendant of the original inhabitants of central and southern Africa

nucleotide—a unit of DNA that consists of a sugar, a phosphate, and a base

nucleus—the control center of a cell

parsing—in forensic anthropology, drawing conclusions about victims from their skeletal remains

pathology—the study of the causes and nature of diseases

physiologist—person who studies the branch of biology dealing with the normal functions of living things

PCR (polymerase chain reaction)—a cloning process used to make a large number of copies of a DNA sequence from very little DNA material for the purpose of DNA fingerprinting

pore—a very small opening in the skin for the release of perspiration

poroscopy—the study of the pore structure of the fingertip as a means of identification

portrait parlé—a French phrase that means "a picture that speaks"

precipitate—a substance separated out of a solution as a solid

precipitin test—the use of blood serums to determine whether a sample of blood is human or from some other animal

RFLP (restriction fragment length polymorphism)—most frequently used process of obtaining DNA fingerprints

saliva—colorless, watery fluid in the mouth

scientific method—logic-based method used by scientists to solve problems, including the forming and testing of hypotheses

semen—fluid produced in the male reproductive organs

serum—the colorless liquid part of blood

species—a group of related organisms that have common characteristics and naturally interbreed

spectroscope—an instrument that produces a microscopic picture of the radiant energy patterns given off by a substance

supraorbital—the bony ridge that makes up the brow

theory of evolution—theory that all existing species of living organisms developed from a few simple forms of life

trace evidence—dust, hairs, threads, and other tiny bits of material used as forensic evidence

vaginal fluid—fluid produced in the female reproductive organs

video skull-face superimposition—the use of video equipment to superimpose a skull onto a photograph for purposes of identification

whorl—in fingerprinting, a skin ridge that circles or turns around another

END NOTES

CHAPTER 1

1. Thorwald, Jurgen. *The Century of the Detective.* New York: Harcourt, Brace & World, Inc., 1964, pp. 12–13.

2. Thorwald, ibid, p. 22.

3. Thorwald, ibid, p. 31.

4. Thorwald, ibid, p. 26.

5. Thorwald, ibid, p. 47.

CHAPTER 2

1. Galton, Francis. "Personal Identification and Description." *Nature,* June 28, 1888. Internet page at URL: <www.iinet.com/market/scafo>.

2. Faulds, Henry. "On the Skin-Furrows of the Hand." *Nature,* October 28, 1880. Internet page at URL: <www.iinet.com/market/scafo>.

3. Faulds, ibid.

4. Faulds, ibid.

5. Thorwald, ibid, p. 59.

6. Chapel, Charles Edward. *Fingerprinting: A Manual of Identification.* New York: Coward McCann, 1941, p. 85.

7. Chapel, ibid, p. 84.

8. Henry, Edward. *Classification and Uses of Finger Prints.* London, England: His Majesty's Stationery Office, 1913. Internet page at URL:<www.iinet.com/market/scafo>.

9. Thorwald, ibid, p. 77.

10. Thorwald, ibid, p. 64.

11. Thorwald, ibid, p. 79.

12. Howe, Sir Ronald. *The Story of Scotland Yard.* New York: Horizon Press, 1966, p. 80.

13. Thorwald, ibid. p. 2.

CHAPTER 3

1. Thorwald, Jurgen. *Crime and Science.* New York: Harcourt, Brace & World, Inc., 1967, p. 33.

2. Thorwald, ibid., p. 32.

3. Thorwald, ibid., p. 40

4. Thorwald, ibid, p. 45.

CHAPTER 4

1. Thorwald, Jurgen. *Crime and Science.* New York: Harcourt, Brace & World, Inc., 1967, p. 182.

2. Thorwald, ibid, p. 286.

3. Thorwald, ibid, pp. 281–282.

4. Evans, Colin. *Casebook of Forensic Detection*. New York: Wiley, 1996, p. 249.

5. Marriner, Brian. *On Death's Bloody Trail*. New York: St. Martin's Press, 1991, p. 175.

CHAPTER 5

1. Joyce, Christopher and Stover, Eric. *Witnesses from the Grave*. New York: Little, Brown and Company, 1991, p. 95.

2. Green, Michelle. "Dr. Clyde Snow Helps Victims of Argentina's 'Dirty War' Bear Witness From Beyond the Grave." *People Weekly*, December 8, 1986, p. 44.

3. Joyce, ibid, p. 161.

4. Joyce, ibid, p. 144.

5. Lander, Eric S. "Use of DNA in Identification." Internet page at URL: <www.mit.edu:8001/esgbio/rdna/landerfinger.html>.

6. Joyce, ibid, p. 217.

7. Green, ibid, p. 112.

8. Joyce, ibid, p. 247.

9. Green, ibid, p. 114.

10. Joyce, ibid, p. 217.

CHAPTER 6

1. Appleyard, Bryan. *Understanding the Present*. New York: Doubleday, 1992, p. 70.

2. Lander, ibid.

3. Jeffreys, Alec. "Career Profile." Internet page at URL: <www.aai.org/genetics/gsa/careers/bro-05.htm>.

4. Chapman, Tim. "From Antarctica to Chernobyl." Internet page at URL: <ci.mond.org/9722/972211. html>. Posted November 17, 1997.

5. Lander, ibid.

6. Lee, Thomas F. *Gene Future.* New York: Plenum Press, 1993, p. 48.

7. Jeffreys, Alec. "Gene Genies." Internet page at URL: <www.abc.net.au/science/sweek/ausprize/walecj. htm>.

8. Jeffreys, ibid.

9. Wambaugh, Joseph. *The Blooding.* New York: William Morrow, 1989, pp. 150–151.

10. Jeffreys, ibid.

11. Wambaugh, ibid, p. 167.

12. Wambaugh, ibid, p. 169.

13. "DNA Fingerprinting and Its Uses." Internet page at URL: <www.cs.bsu.edu/~anuradha/dna.html>.

14. Levy, Harlan. *And the Blood Cried Out.* New York: BasicBooks, 1996, p. 50.

15. Kolata, Gina. "Chief Says Panel Backs Courts' Use of a Genetic Test." *New York Times*, April 15, 1992, p. A1.

16. Lander, ibid.

17. Jeffreys, Sir Alec. "Sir Alec Jeffreys on DNA Profiling and Mini-satellites." *Science Watch*, April, 1995, p. 4.

SELECTED BIBLIOGRAPHY

Works preceded by an asterisk (*) are recommended for young readers.

CHAPTER 1

*Gribble, Leonard. *Stories of Famous Detectives*. New York: Hill and Wang, 1963.

*Kind, Stuart and Michael Overman. *Science Against Crime*. New York: Nature and Science Library, 1972.

*Lane, Brian. *Crime & Detection*. New York: Alfred A. Knopf, 1998.

*Thomas, Peggy. *Talking Bones*. New York: Facts On File, 1995.

Thorwald, Jurgen. *The Century of the Detective*. New York: Harcourt, Brace & World, Inc., 1964.

CHAPTER 2

Chapel, Charles Edward. *Fingerprinting: A Manual of Identification*. New York: Coward McCann, 1941.

Faulds, Henry. "On the Skin-Furrows of the Hand." *Nature*, October 28, 1880.

Galton, Francis. "Personal Identification and Description." *Nature*, June 28, 1888.

"General Information About Fingerprints." Internet page at URL: <www.iinet.com/market/scafo>.

Henry, Edward. *Classification and Uses of Finger Prints*. London: His Majesty's Stationery Office, 1913.

*Howe, Sir Ronald. *The Story of Scotland Yard*. New York: Horizon Press, 1966.

Moenssens, Andre. *Fingerprints and the Law*. New York: Chilton Book Company, 1969.

*Twain, Mark. *Pudd'nhead Wilson*. New York: Grosset & Dunlap, 1989.

CHAPTER 3

*Abbot, David (ed). *The Biographical Dictionary of Scientists, Biologists*. New York: Peter Bedrick Books, 1984.

*Evans, Colin. *The Casebook of Forensic Detection*. New York: Wiley, 1996.

McMurray, Emily (ed). *Notable Twentieth-Century Scientists*. Detroit, MI: Gale Research, 1995.

*Silverstein, Herma. *Threads of Evidence*. New York: Twenty-First Century Books, 1996.

Thorwald, Jurgen. *Crime and Science*. New York: Harcourt, Brace & World, 1967.

CHAPTER 4

Almirall, Jose and Kenneth Furton. "The Importance of Standards in Forensic Science." *Standardization News*, Volume 23, Number 4, April, 1995.

*Doyle, Arthur Conan. *A Study in Scarlet*. New York: Oxford University Press, 1994.

O'Hara, Charles E. and Gregory L. O'Hara. *Fundamentals of Criminal Investigation*. Springfield, Illinois: Charles C. Thomas, 1994.

Saferstein, Richard. *Criminalistics*. Englewood Cliffs, New Jersey: Prentice Hall, 1995.

*Smith, Sydney. *Mostly Murder*. New York: David McKay Company, 1959

CHAPTER 5

*Green, Michelle. "Dr. Clyde Snow Helps Victims of Argentina's 'Dirty War' Bear Witness from Beyond the Grave." *People Weekly*, December 8, 1986.

*Huyghe, Patrick. "No Bone Unturned." *Discover*, December, 1988.

*Jackson, Donna. *The Bone Detectives*. Boston: Little, Brown and Company, 1996.

*Jones, Charlotte Foltz. *Fingerprints and Talking Bones*. New York: Delacorte, 1997.

*Joyce, Christopher and Eric Stover. *Witnesses from the Grave*. Boston: Little, Brown and Company, 1991.

Marriner, Brian. *On Death's Bloody Trail*. New York: St. Martin's Press, 1991.

*Stover, Eric. "The Grave at Vukovar." *Smithsonian*, March, 1997.

CHAPTER 6

"DNA Fingerprinting and Its Uses." Internet page at URL: <www.cs.bsu.edu/~anuradha/dna.html>.

Jeffreys, Alec. "Career Profile." Internet page at URL: <www.aai.org/genetics/gsa/careers/bro-05.htm>.

Jeffreys, Alec. "Gene Genies." Internet page at URL: <www.abc.net.au/science/sweek/ausprize/walecj.htm>.

Jeffreys, Sir Alec. "Sir Alec Jeffreys on DNA Profiling and Mini-satellites." *Science Watch*, April, 1995.

*Lampton, Christopher. *DNA Fingerprinting*. New York: Franklin Watts, 1991.

Lander, Eric S. "Use of DNA in Identification." Internet page at URL: <esg-www.mit.edu:8001/esgbio/rdna/landerfinger.html>.

Lee, Thomas F. *Gene Future*. New York: Plenum Press, 1993.

Levy, Harlan. *And the Blood Cried Out*. New York: Basic-Books, 1996.

Wambaugh, Joseph. *The Blooding*. New York: William Morrow, 1989.

ONLINE SITES

A great deal of information on forensic science is available on the World Wide Web. You can use a search engine, such as Yahoo, Alta Vista, and Excite, to call up lists of Web sites. Try some of the following key words:

- forensic science
- DNA
- fingerprints
- blood typing
- forensic anthropology
- crime laboratory
- Sherlock Holmes
- FBI
- criminology

The following is a list of Web sites dealing with various aspects of forensic science. Because Internet sites are not always permanent, they may change addresses or even cease to exist over time. The sites that follow have been in existence for quite some time.

Discovery Channel Online
http://www.discovery.com
This is the Internet site of the science-oriented cable-TV channel. Search the site for news and articles on forensic science.

Evidence: The True Witness
http://www.library.advanced.org/17049/gather/
Detailed information about various aspects of forensic science, including fingerprinting, DNA fingerprinting, and forensic anthropology. Includes information on careers in forensic science.

The Case.com
http://www.TheCase.com
Dedicated to the idea that "Mysteries are great for teaching critical thinking, reading, and writing skills." Features mini-mysteries for visitors to read and solve, a "History of the Mystery" quiz, and a writing contest for aspiring mystery writers.

Zeno's Forensic Page
http://www.users.bart.nl/~geradts/forensic.html
List of links to dozens of sites dealing with all aspects of forensic science.

Sherlockian Information
http://www.geocities.com/~sherlockian/link_4_1_yop.html
Links to dozens of sites dealing with Sherlock Holmes, Arthur Conan Doyle's fictional detective, who has inspired detectives and forensic scientists for more than a century.

Holmes's Place

http://www3.nf.sympatico.ca/dave.pack/holmes.html
Includes the full text of all Sherlock Holmes's adventures.

DNA Forensics: Crime

http://www.people.virginia.edu/~rjh9u/forenscr.html
See if you can figure out which one of the seven suspects' DNA fingerprints matches the one taken from a bloodstain at the scene of the crime.

The Simpson File Transcripts

http://www.mbay.net/~walraven/simpson/simpson.html
Complete transcripts of all 9 months of testimony from "the trial of the century," in which DNA evidence was the key. Includes juror interviews, witness lists, and the verdict.

PLACES TO VISIT

Would you like to see exhibits depicting the history of forensic science? Here are some places you can visit in different parts of the country.

American Police Center and Museum
1717 South State Street
Chicago, Illinois 60616-1215

American Police Hall of Fame and Museum
3801 Biscayne Blvd.
Miami, Florida 33137

Cleveland Police Historical Society and Museum Justice Center
1300 Ontario Street
Cleveland, Ohio 44113

Criminal Justice Hall of Fame
5400 Broad River Road
Columbia, South Carolina 29210

J. Edgar Hoover FBI Building
10th Street and Pennsylvania Avenue, Northwest
Washington, D.C. 20535

Mystery Festival
Lawrence Hall of Science
University of California
Berkeley, California 94720

Phoenix Police Museum
Barrister Place Building
101 South Central Avenue, Suite 100
Phoenix, Arizona 85004

Texas Ranger Museum and Hall of Fame
Exit 335B, I-35 and University Park
P.O. Box 2570
Waco, Texas 76702-2570

INDEX

ABOUT THE AUTHOR

Ron Fridell has been writing since his college days at Northwestern University where he earned a Master's Degree in Radio, TV, Film. He has written for radio, TV, newspapers, and textbooks. He taught English as a second language while a member of the Peace Corps in Bangkok, Thailand. He lives in Evanston, Illinois, with his wife Patricia and their dog, an Australian shepherd named Madeline. His blood type is A positive.